Mastering SQL: Query Databases Like a Pro

A Step-by-Step Guide to Writing and Optimizing SQL Queries

BOOZMAN RICHARD

BOOKER BLUNT

Table of Content

TABLE OF CONTENTS

INTRODUCTION

Mastering SQL: Query Databases Like a Pro is designed to provide a comprehensive guide for anyone seeking to master the art of querying and managing databases using Structured Query Language (SQL). Whether you're a beginner just starting your journey with databases or an experienced developer looking to enhance your skills, this book is crafted to take you through every essential concept, from the fundamentals to advanced techniques, empowering you to efficiently manage, analyze, and optimize SQL databases.

In today's data-driven world, SQL remains the standard language for interacting with relational databases. Every business, application, and service that manages large datasets relies on SQL for retrieving, updating, and manipulating data. Databases power everything from e-commerce websites to financial systems, social networks, and beyond. The ability to write efficient and effective SQL queries is crucial for anyone working in fields such as software development, data analysis, business intelligence, or database administration.

8

This book goes beyond simply teaching SQL syntax. We emphasize practical, real-world applications of SQL to solve everyday problems, optimize database performance, and streamline data processing. By understanding how to craft well-optimized queries and design robust, efficient databases, you'll be prepared to tackle complex data challenges with confidence and precision.

What You Will Learn

1. The Fundamentals of SQL You'll start with the basics of SQL, including creating databases and tables, and writing simple queries to retrieve and manipulate data. We'll dive into core SQL operations like `SELECT`, `INSERT`, `UPDATE`, and `DELETE`, and explore how to filter, sort, and aggregate data. By the end of these foundational sections, you will have a solid understanding of how SQL works and how to interact with a relational database.

2. Advanced Querying Techniques Once you've mastered the basics, you'll move on to more advanced topics such as complex joins, nested queries, and subqueries. We'll explain how to combine data from multiple tables efficiently, filter and group data, and use functions and expressions to manipulate the results. These techniques are essential for working with larger and more complex datasets, and are commonly used in real-world business scenarios.

3. Data Analysis and Reporting SQL isn't just about data retrieval—it's also a powerful tool for data analysis. In this book, we'll show you how to use SQL to generate meaningful reports, calculate key metrics, and perform in-depth data analysis. You'll learn how to aggregate data, create complex reports, and leverage SQL's built-in functions for analyzing trends, calculating averages, totals, and percentages, and much more.

4. Database Design and Optimization SQL is not only about writing queries but also about designing databases that are efficient and scalable. This book covers the best practices for database design, including normalization, indexing, and how to ensure data integrity. We'll also teach you how to optimize queries for better performance, a crucial skill for managing large datasets and ensuring that your database runs smoothly under heavy loads.

5. Security and Best Practices As databases store some of the most sensitive information, security is a major concern. This book includes an entire section on securing SQL queries, preventing SQL injection attacks, and using best practices for managing user permissions and data access. By the end of this section, you will understand how to protect your databases from potential security risks.

6. The Future of SQL and Database Technologies Finally, we'll discuss the future of SQL in an evolving tech ecosystem. SQL is still the cornerstone of relational databases, but with the rise of **NoSQL** databases, cloud platforms, and big data technologies, the database landscape is changing rapidly. We'll explore how SQL fits into the modern world of data management and what emerging trends like cloud databases, hybrid systems, and machine learning mean for SQL developers.

Why This Book?

There are countless resources available for learning SQL, but what sets this book apart is its practical approach. Each chapter is packed with real-world examples and hands-on exercises that allow you to apply what you've learned immediately. We don't just provide abstract examples; instead, we present use cases and scenarios you might encounter in a real job setting—whether you're querying sales data for a business, managing an e-commerce site, or analyzing customer information.

You won't just read about SQL—you'll work with it. Every concept comes with step-by-step explanations and exercises to reinforce your learning. The book is structured progressively, starting with simple queries and moving to more complex techniques, so you can build your knowledge and skills at a comfortable pace.

Whether you're working on small personal projects, enterprise-level applications, or large-scale databases, the skills you'll acquire from this book will be directly applicable to your work.

Who Should Read This Book?

- **Beginners**: If you're new to SQL and databases, this book is a great place to start. You'll learn everything from the very basics to more advanced topics, with clear explanations and practical examples.
- **Developers and Programmers**: If you're already a software developer but need to work with databases, this book will provide the SQL skills you need to interact with data effectively, optimize your queries, and enhance your applications.
- **Data Analysts and Business Intelligence Professionals**: For those working with data on a

daily basis, understanding SQL is crucial. This book will teach you how to use SQL for data analysis, generate reports, and perform key business operations.

- **Database Administrators**: If you're tasked with maintaining and optimizing databases, this book will help you understand how to ensure data integrity, optimize performance, and secure your systems.

- **Anyone Looking to Transition into Data Science**: SQL is a foundational skill for any data scientist. This book will give you the tools to interact with and analyze data, providing a stepping stone toward more advanced data science techniques.

The Journey Ahead

In the following chapters, we will guide you through every aspect of SQL and database management, starting with the fundamentals and gradually building up to advanced topics. By the end of this book, you'll have the knowledge and practical skills to design, query, and optimize databases, handle complex data analysis tasks, and ensure data security.

Whether you're looking to enhance your career or gain the skills to work with data in your personal projects, **Mastering**

SQL will give you the tools you need to succeed. Let's begin your journey into the world of SQL!

CHAPTER 1

INTRODUCTION TO SQL

Overview of SQL and its Importance in Modern Databases

SQL, which stands for Structured Query Language, is the standard language used to communicate with and manage data stored in relational databases. It allows you to retrieve, update, delete, and manipulate data efficiently. SQL has been around since the 1970s and remains a fundamental tool for anyone working with databases, whether for small-scale applications or large enterprise systems.

In modern databases, SQL serves as the bridge between the user and the data. It helps businesses, organizations, and developers interact with data in an organized and structured way. The significance of SQL lies in its ability to work seamlessly across various database systems, such as MySQL, PostgreSQL, Oracle, and SQL Server, making it an essential skill for data analysts, software developers, and database administrators.

SQL is essential for:

- **Data Retrieval:** It allows you to query and retrieve specific data that you need from large datasets.

- **Data Management:** SQL supports various operations for managing data, such as inserting new data, updating existing records, and deleting outdated or incorrect information.
- **Data Integrity:** It ensures data consistency, reliability, and security through features like constraints, triggers, and transactions.

Explanation of Databases, Tables, and Records

To fully understand SQL, it's important to first understand the foundational elements of databases:

1. **Database**: A database is a collection of data that is organized and stored electronically. It can contain multiple tables and other objects like views, indexes, and stored procedures. A database is often designed for a specific application, such as managing customer data for a business or handling inventory for a warehouse.

2. **Table**: A table in a database is a collection of rows and columns, where each row represents a single record, and each column represents an attribute or a field of that record. For example, a table might store information about employees, with columns like "Employee ID," "First Name," "Last Name," and "Date of Birth."

3. **Record (or Row)**: A record is a single, complete set of data within a table, represented by a row. Each record

corresponds to an entity, such as an individual employee, customer, or product. For example, in a table of employees, each row would represent one employee's details.

4. **Field (or Column)**: A column is a vertical collection of data that represents a specific attribute across all records in the table. Each column is defined by a data type (such as integer, string, or date), and each field within a column contains a piece of information corresponding to the attribute.

Real-World Example: Using SQL in a Small Business to Manage Customer Data

Let's take a look at a real-world example of using SQL in a small business to manage customer data. Suppose you're running a local bakery, and you want to keep track of customer orders. You'd use a database to store and manage this information.

1. **Create a Customer Table:** You would create a table named "Customers" to store essential details like customer names, contact information, and order history. This could look like the following SQL query:

sql

```
CREATE TABLE Customers (
    CustomerID INT PRIMARY KEY,
```

```
FirstName VARCHAR(50),
LastName VARCHAR(50),
Email VARCHAR(100),
PhoneNumber VARCHAR(15)
);
```

In this query:

- o CustomerID is an integer and serves as the primary key, which uniquely identifies each customer.
- o FirstName and LastName are string fields (VARCHAR), each with a maximum length of 50 characters.
- o Email is a string field that holds the customer's email address.
- o PhoneNumber stores the customer's contact number.

2. **Insert Customer Data:** After creating the table, you can insert records (rows) into the "Customers" table. Each record will represent an individual customer:

sql

```
INSERT INTO Customers (CustomerID,
FirstName, LastName, Email, PhoneNumber)
VALUES (1, 'John', 'Doe',
'johndoe@example.com', '555-1234');
```

18

This query adds a new customer record with John Doe's details. You can add as many customers as you need by repeating similar INSERT queries.

3. **Retrieve Customer Information:** Once you have a collection of customer data, you can use SQL queries to retrieve specific information. For example, if you want to find the contact details of a customer based on their name, you can use a SELECT statement:

sql

```
SELECT FirstName, LastName, Email,
PhoneNumber
FROM Customers
WHERE LastName = 'Doe';
```

This query retrieves the first name, last name, email, and phone number of all customers whose last name is "Doe."

4. **Updating Customer Data:** If a customer changes their email address or phone number, you can update their information using the UPDATE statement:

sql

```
UPDATE Customers
SET Email = 'john.doe@newdomain.com',
PhoneNumber = '555-6789'
```

19

```
WHERE CustomerID = 1;
```

This query updates the email and phone number for the customer with `CustomerID = 1`.

5. **Deleting Customer Data:** If a customer decides to stop using your bakery's services, and you no longer need their information, you can remove their record using the `DELETE` statement:

sql

```
DELETE FROM Customers
WHERE CustomerID = 1;
```

This query removes the customer with `CustomerID = 1` from the "Customers" table.

Summary

In this chapter, you learned the basics of SQL, including its importance in modern databases, and how databases, tables, and records work. Through the example of managing customer data for a small business, you saw how SQL allows you to create tables, insert records, retrieve and update data, and even delete records as necessary. By mastering these foundational skills, you're on your way to becoming proficient in SQL and effectively managing data in relational databases.

CHAPTER 2

SETTING UP YOUR SQL ENVIRONMENT

Installing SQL Tools (MySQL, PostgreSQL, SQLite, etc.)

Before you can start writing SQL queries, you need to install the necessary tools to interact with a database. There are several popular database systems, each with its installation process, but all of them will allow you to run SQL queries and manage your data. In this chapter, we'll cover three of the most commonly used SQL database systems: MySQL, PostgreSQL, and SQLite.

1. MySQL Installation: MySQL is one of the most widely used relational database management systems (RDBMS). It is open-source, fast, and reliable.

- **Steps to install MySQL**:
    1. Go to the MySQL website and download the installer for your operating system.
    2. Run the installer, and follow the prompts.
    3. During installation, you'll be asked to set up a root password. This password will be used to access the MySQL server.

4. Once installed, open the **MySQL Workbench** (a graphical user interface for MySQL) to manage your databases, or you can use the command-line interface (CLI).

5. To test the installation, open MySQL Workbench and log in using the root password you set up. You can now start creating databases and running SQL queries.

2. PostgreSQL Installation: PostgreSQL is another popular open-source database system known for its scalability and support for advanced features like JSON and custom data types.

- **Steps to install PostgreSQL:**

    1. Visit the PostgreSQL official website and download the installer for your operating system.

    2. Run the installer and follow the installation wizard.

    3. Set a password for the PostgreSQL superuser (the default superuser is named `postgres`).

    4. After installation, use **pgAdmin**, a graphical management tool for PostgreSQL, to interact with your database.

    5. Test the installation by logging into pgAdmin or using the command-line tool `psql` with the superuser credentials.

3. SQLite Installation: SQLite is a self-contained, file-based SQL database engine. It is easy to set up and does not require a separate server process, making it ideal for smaller applications or testing.

- **Steps to install SQLite**:
    1. Go to the SQLite download page and download the appropriate file for your operating system.
    2. Extract the downloaded file to a folder on your computer.
    3. Open a terminal or command prompt window and navigate to the folder where SQLite is located.
    4. Type `sqlite3` to launch the SQLite command-line interface (CLI).
    5. You can now create a new database by typing `sqlite3 mydatabase.db`, which will create and open a new SQLite database file named `mydatabase.db`.

Connecting to a Database Using a Local Server

After installing SQL tools, the next step is to connect to your database using a local server. This is necessary so that you can start interacting with your data. Below is how you can connect to your SQL database using MySQL, PostgreSQL, and SQLite.

1. Connecting to MySQL Database:

To connect to MySQL via the command-line interface (CLI), follow these steps:

- Open your terminal or command prompt.
- Type the following command to connect to the MySQL server:

```bash
mysql -u root -p
```

This tells MySQL to connect using the `root` user and prompts you for the password.

- Once logged in, you can run SQL commands such as creating databases, creating tables, or querying data.

To connect via **MySQL Workbench**:

- Open MySQL Workbench.
- Create a new connection by clicking on the + symbol next to "MySQL Connections."
- Enter the connection details such as host (usually `localhost`), username (usually `root`), and password.
- Click "Test Connection" to verify that the connection is successful, then click "OK."

2. Connecting to PostgreSQL Database:

To connect to PostgreSQL via the CLI:

- Open your terminal or command prompt.
- Type the following command to log in to PostgreSQL using the `postgres` superuser:

```bash

psql -U postgres
```

After typing this, you'll be prompted to enter the password you set up during installation.

- Once logged in, you can use SQL commands to interact with the database.

To connect via **pgAdmin**:

- Open **pgAdmin**.
- Create a new connection by clicking on the "Add New Server" icon.
- Enter the server name, connection host (usually `localhost`), and the superuser credentials.
- Click "Save" to connect to the database and manage it through the graphical interface.

3. Connecting to SQLite Database:

SQLite does not require a server process. You can simply open the SQLite database file directly from the command line:

- Open the terminal or command prompt.
- Navigate to the folder where your database file is located (or create a new one).
- Type the following command to open the SQLite database:

```bash
sqlite3 mydatabase.db
```

This opens the SQLite database `mydatabase.db` for querying and modification.

If you're using an SQLite database in an application, you can integrate it directly into your app through libraries and APIs provided by your programming language.

Real-World Example: Setting Up SQL on Your Computer to Work with a Sample Database

In this example, we'll set up a MySQL database on your computer to work with a sample database for managing a fictional bookstore's inventory. The process will involve installing MySQL, creating a sample database, and performing basic SQL queries.

1. **Install MySQL**: Follow the steps from earlier to install MySQL on your computer and connect to the MySQL Workbench.

2. **Create the Sample Database**: After connecting to MySQL, create a new database for the bookstore inventory:

sql

```
CREATE DATABASE Bookstore;
```

3. **Create Tables**: Within the `Bookstore` database, create a table for storing book details such as title, author, and price:

sql

```
USE Bookstore;

CREATE TABLE Books (
    BookID INT PRIMARY KEY AUTO_INCREMENT,
    Title VARCHAR(100),
    Author VARCHAR(100),
    Price DECIMAL(8, 2)
);
```

4. **Insert Sample Data**: Now, let's insert a few records into the `Books` table:

27

sql

```
INSERT INTO Books (Title, Author, Price)
VALUES ('The Great Gatsby', 'F. Scott
Fitzgerald', 10.99),
       ('1984', 'George Orwell', 8.99),
       ('To Kill a Mockingbird', 'Harper
Lee', 7.49);
```

5. **Query Data**: Retrieve all the books in the Books table:

sql

```
SELECT * FROM Books;
```

6. **Update Data**: Suppose the price of "1984" changes. You can update the price like this:

sql

```
UPDATE Books
SET Price = 9.99
WHERE Title = '1984';
```

7. **Delete Data**: If you need to delete a book record from the database, you can do so using:

sql

```
DELETE FROM Books
```

```
WHERE Title = 'To Kill a Mockingbird';
```

By following these steps, you've successfully set up MySQL, created a database, and started querying data. You can now practice running SQL queries on this sample database and apply your skills to more complex tasks.

Summary

In this chapter, you learned how to install and set up popular SQL database tools like MySQL, PostgreSQL, and SQLite. You also connected to a database using a local server, and followed a real-world example of setting up a MySQL database to manage a bookstore's inventory. This foundation is essential as you move forward with more advanced SQL concepts.

CHAPTER 3

WRITING YOUR FIRST SQL QUERY

Basic SELECT Queries to Retrieve Data from a Table

The SELECT statement is the most commonly used SQL query. It is the starting point for interacting with data in a database. With the SELECT statement, you can retrieve data from one or more tables.

The basic structure of a SELECT query looks like this:

sql

```
SELECT column1, column2, column3
FROM table_name;
```

- SELECT is the keyword that tells the database you want to retrieve data.
- column1, column2, column3 are the names of the columns from which you want to retrieve data.
- FROM specifies the table from which you want to retrieve the data.

If you want to retrieve all the columns in a table, you can use the * wildcard:

```sql
sql

SELECT * FROM table_name;
```

This will return all columns for every record in the table.

Example:

Let's assume you have a table called `Customers` with the following columns:

- `CustomerID`
- `FirstName`
- `LastName`
- `Email`

If you want to retrieve the first and last names of all customers, you would use this query:

```sql
sql

SELECT FirstName, LastName
FROM Customers;
```

This will return a list of all customers with their first and last names.

Filtering Data Using the WHERE Clause

In most cases, you will need to filter the data based on certain conditions. You can do this with the WHERE clause. The WHERE clause allows you to specify conditions that must be met for a record to be included in the results.

The basic structure for using WHERE is:

sql

```
SELECT column1, column2
FROM table_name
WHERE condition;
```

- The condition could be a comparison or logical operation that the data must meet. You can use operators like =, >, <, >=, <=, <>, BETWEEN, IN, LIKE, and more.

Example:

Let's say you want to retrieve the information for customers who live in a specific city. Assume there's a column City in your Customers table. To get the data for customers in the city of "New York," you would write:

sql

```
SELECT FirstName, LastName, City
```

```
FROM Customers
WHERE City = 'New York';
```

This query filters the data to only include customers who live in New York.

Operators in WHERE Clause:

- =: Equal to
- >: Greater than
- <: Less than
- >=: Greater than or equal to
- <=: Less than or equal to
- <>: Not equal to
- BETWEEN: To specify a range of values
- IN: To match against a list of values
- LIKE: To search for a pattern

For example:

- Retrieving customers who are older than 30 years:

sql

```
SELECT FirstName, LastName, Age
FROM Customers
WHERE Age > 30;
```

- Retrieving customers whose last name starts with "D":

sql

```
SELECT FirstName, LastName
FROM Customers
WHERE LastName LIKE 'D%';
```

Real-World Example: Retrieving Customer Orders from a Database

In a real-world scenario, you may have a Customers table and an Orders table in your database. Let's assume the following structure for the tables:

- **Customers** table:
    - CustomerID (Primary Key)
    - FirstName
    - LastName
    - Email
- **Orders** table:
    - OrderID (Primary Key)
    - CustomerID (Foreign Key to Customers table)
    - OrderDate
    - TotalAmount

You want to retrieve all customer orders, including the customer's name and the total amount of each order. Here's how you would write the SQL query:

Step 1: Using SELECT to retrieve data

```sql
sql

SELECT    Orders.OrderID,    Customers.FirstName,
Customers.LastName,              Orders.OrderDate,
Orders.TotalAmount
FROM Orders
JOIN    Customers    ON    Orders.CustomerID    =
Customers.CustomerID;
```

In this query:

- We are selecting the `OrderID`, `FirstName`, `LastName`, `OrderDate`, and `TotalAmount` columns.
- The `JOIN` clause connects the `Orders` table with the `Customers` table based on the `CustomerID` field. This way, we can display the customer's name alongside their order details.

Step 2: Filtering the data

Suppose you only want to see orders that were placed after January 1st, 2025. You can use the `WHERE` clause to filter the results:

```sql
sql

SELECT    Orders.OrderID,    Customers.FirstName,
Customers.LastName,              Orders.OrderDate,
Orders.TotalAmount
```

```
FROM Orders
JOIN   Customers   ON   Orders.CustomerID   =
Customers.CustomerID
WHERE Orders.OrderDate > '2025-01-01';
```

This query will return only those orders where the OrderDate is after January 1, 2025.

Step 3: Sorting the results

You may want to sort the results by OrderDate in descending order (most recent orders first). You can use the ORDER BY clause:

sql

```
SELECT   Orders.OrderID,   Customers.FirstName,
Customers.LastName,          Orders.OrderDate,
Orders.TotalAmount
FROM Orders
JOIN   Customers   ON   Orders.CustomerID   =
Customers.CustomerID
WHERE Orders.OrderDate > '2025-01-01'
ORDER BY Orders.OrderDate DESC;
```

This query retrieves the orders placed after January 1, 2025, and sorts them by the OrderDate in descending order.

Example Output:

OrderID	FirstName	LastName	OrderDate	TotalAmount
101	John	Doe	2025-02-15	150.50
102	Jane	Smith	2025-03-20	200.00
103	Michael	Johnson	2025-04-05	99.99

This output shows a list of customer orders placed after January 1st, 2025, including the customer's name, order date, and total amount.

Summary

In this chapter, you learned how to write your first SQL query using the SELECT statement to retrieve data from a table. You also learned how to filter results using the WHERE clause and apply operators to filter data based on conditions. Through a real-world example of retrieving customer orders, you saw how to join tables and use additional clauses such as ORDER BY and WHERE to refine your query results. These basic skills are essential for working with SQL and form the foundation for more advanced querying techniques.

CHAPTER 4

UNDERSTANDING DATA TYPES AND OPERATORS

Different Data Types: Strings, Integers, Dates, etc.

SQL is used to interact with different types of data, and understanding how data is stored and manipulated is essential to writing effective queries. Each column in a table is defined with a specific **data type**, which determines the kind of data it can store. The main data types in SQL can be classified into several categories:

1. String Data Types: String data types are used to store text values. The most common types are:

- **VARCHAR(n)**: A variable-length string with a maximum length of n characters. For example, VARCHAR(100) can store any string of up to 100 characters.
- **CHAR(n)**: A fixed-length string. If the string is shorter than n characters, it will be padded with spaces. For example, CHAR(50) will always store 50 characters, even if fewer are entered.

- **TEXT**: A string data type used to store larger amounts of text. Typically used for descriptions or comments.

Example:

sql

```
CREATE TABLE Customers (
    CustomerID INT PRIMARY KEY,
    FirstName VARCHAR(50),
    LastName VARCHAR(50),
    Email TEXT
);
```

2. Numeric Data Types: Numeric data types store numbers, either integers or decimal values.

- **INT**: Stores whole numbers. Example: INT can hold values like 1, 2, 100, etc.
- **DECIMAL(p, s)**: Stores fixed-point numbers with a specified precision p and scale s. Example: DECIMAL(8, 2) can store values like 12345.67, where 8 is the total number of digits, and 2 is the number of digits after the decimal point.
- **FLOAT** and **DOUBLE**: These types store approximate floating-point numbers, useful for calculations that require a high degree of precision.

Example:

```sql
sql


CREATE TABLE Products (
    ProductID INT PRIMARY KEY,
    ProductName VARCHAR(100),
    Price DECIMAL(10, 2)
);
```

3. Date and Time Data Types: These data types are used to store dates and times.

- **DATE**: Stores a date in the format `YYYY-MM-DD`. Example: `2025-04-30`.
- **TIME**: Stores time values in `HH:MM:SS` format.
- **DATETIME** or **TIMESTAMP**: Stores both date and time in the format `YYYY-MM-DD HH:MM:SS`. Often used to track when a record is created or updated.

Example:

```sql
sql


CREATE TABLE Orders (
    OrderID INT PRIMARY KEY,
    OrderDate DATETIME,
    CustomerID INT,
    TotalAmount DECIMAL(10, 2)
```

```
);
```

4. Boolean Data Types:

- **BOOLEAN**: Stores truth values (true or false). In some databases like MySQL, this is implemented as `TINYINT(1)` with values 0 (false) or 1 (true).

Example:

```
sql
```

```
CREATE TABLE Products (
    ProductID INT PRIMARY KEY,
    ProductName VARCHAR(100),
    IsAvailable BOOLEAN
);
```

Arithmetic Operators and Comparison Operators

1. Arithmetic Operators: SQL allows you to perform mathematical calculations using arithmetic operators. These operators are used to calculate values and update records in a table.

- + (Addition): Adds two values.
- - (Subtraction): Subtracts one value from another.
- * (Multiplication): Multiplies two values.
- / (Division): Divides one value by another.
- % (Modulus): Returns the remainder of a division.

41

Example: If you want to calculate the total cost of multiple products in an order (with quantity and price), you can use arithmetic operators:

sql

```
SELECT ProductName, Price, Quantity, (Price *
Quantity) AS TotalCost
FROM OrderDetails;
```

In this query, `Price * Quantity` calculates the total cost for each product in the order.

2. Comparison Operators: Comparison operators are used to compare two values and return a Boolean result (TRUE or FALSE). These are essential when filtering data with the WHERE clause.

- = (Equal to): Returns TRUE if both values are equal.
- <> or != (Not equal to): Returns TRUE if the values are not equal.
- > (Greater than): Returns TRUE if the left value is greater than the right value.
- < (Less than): Returns TRUE if the left value is less than the right value.
- >= (Greater than or equal to): Returns TRUE if the left value is greater than or equal to the right value.

- **<=** (Less than or equal to): Returns TRUE if the left value is less than or equal to the right value.
- **BETWEEN**: Checks if a value is within a range.
- **IN**: Checks if a value is in a list of values.
- **LIKE**: Checks if a value matches a pattern.
- **IS NULL**: Checks if a value is NULL (i.e., not defined).

Example: To find all customers whose total orders are greater than $100:

```sql

SELECT    CustomerID,    SUM(TotalAmount)    AS
TotalSpent
FROM Orders
GROUP BY CustomerID
HAVING SUM(TotalAmount) > 100;
```

This query uses the HAVING clause to filter customers whose total spending is greater than 100.

Real-World Example: Calculating Total Sales from an E-commerce Database

In an e-commerce scenario, let's say you have two tables: Orders and OrderDetails.

- **Orders** table:
  - o   OrderID

- o   CustomerID
- o   OrderDate
- o   TotalAmount
- **OrderDetails** table:
  - o   OrderDetailID
  - o   OrderID
  - o   ProductID
  - o   Quantity
  - o   Price

To calculate the total sales for a specific date range, you can join the Orders and OrderDetails tables, then use the SUM function to calculate the total sales amount.

sql

```
SELECT              SUM(OrderDetails.Price      *
OrderDetails.Quantity) AS TotalSales
FROM Orders
JOIN   OrderDetails   ON   Orders.OrderID   =
OrderDetails.OrderID
WHERE Orders.OrderDate BETWEEN '2025-01-01' AND
'2025-04-01';
```

In this query:

- We join the Orders and OrderDetails tables based on the OrderID.

- We use the SUM function to calculate the total sales, multiplying the Price by the Quantity for each order item.
- We filter the results to include only orders between January 1, 2025, and April 1, 2025.

This will give us the total sales for the specified period.

Output Example:

TotalSales

12500.50

This result shows that the total sales from January 1, 2025, to April 1, 2025, amount to $12,500.50.

Summary

In this chapter, you learned about the different data types in SQL, such as strings, integers, decimals, dates, and booleans, and how each one is used to store different kinds of data. You also explored the basic arithmetic operators (e.g., addition, subtraction, multiplication) and comparison operators (e.g., equal to, greater than, between) that are used to manipulate and filter data in queries. Finally, through a real-world example, you saw how to calculate total sales from an e-commerce database, applying these concepts to real business needs. These skills will be foundational as you begin working with more complex data analysis and reporting tasks in SQL.

CHAPTER 5

SORTING AND FILTERING DATA

Using ORDER BY to Sort Results

When working with large datasets, it's often important to sort the results of your SQL queries. Sorting helps you organize data in a way that's meaningful, making it easier to interpret and analyze. The ORDER BY clause is used to sort the result set of a query based on one or more columns, either in ascending (ASC) or descending (DESC) order.

The basic structure of the ORDER BY clause is:

sql

```
SELECT column1, column2
FROM table_name
ORDER BY column1 [ASC | DESC];
```

- ORDER BY: Tells SQL to sort the result set.
- column1: The column(s) to sort the data by.
- [ASC | DESC]: Specifies the sorting order. ASC stands for ascending (from low to high or A to Z) and DESC stands for descending (from high to low or Z to A). If you don't specify an order, the default is ascending.

47

Example:

Let's say you have a `Products` table with the following columns:

- `ProductID`
- `ProductName`
- `Price`
- `AvailabilityStatus`

You want to sort the products by price in ascending order:

sql

```
SELECT ProductName, Price
FROM Products
ORDER BY Price ASC;
```

This query retrieves the list of product names and prices, sorted by price from lowest to highest.

Example with Descending Order:

If you want to sort the products by price in descending order (highest to lowest), you can use:

sql

```
SELECT ProductName, Price
FROM Products
ORDER BY Price DESC;
```

You can also sort by multiple columns. For example, if you want to sort first by `Price` in ascending order, and if there's a tie, then by `ProductName` alphabetically:

sql

```
SELECT ProductName, Price
FROM Products
ORDER BY Price ASC, ProductName ASC;
```

This sorts the products by price in ascending order, and within the same price range, it sorts alphabetically by product name.

Using WHERE to Filter Data Based on Conditions

The `WHERE` clause is used to filter records based on specific conditions. This allows you to retrieve only the data that meets certain criteria, making your queries more efficient and targeted.

The basic syntax for the `WHERE` clause is:

sql

```
SELECT column1, column2
FROM table_name
WHERE condition;
```

- `WHERE`: Tells SQL to filter the results.

- `condition`: The condition that must be true for the row to be included in the result set.

Common Comparison Operators in WHERE:

- =: Equal to
- <> or !=: Not equal to
- >: Greater than
- <: Less than
- >=: Greater than or equal to
- <=: Less than or equal to
- `BETWEEN`: A range of values
- `IN`: A list of values
- `LIKE`: Pattern matching

Example:

Let's say you want to retrieve all products that are available in stock (assuming `AvailabilityStatus` is a column that indicates whether a product is available or not):

sql

```
SELECT ProductName, AvailabilityStatus
FROM Products
WHERE AvailabilityStatus = 'In Stock';
```

This query will return only the products that are marked as "In Stock."

Example with Numerical Filtering:

You might also want to filter products based on price. Let's say you want to find products that cost more than $50:

sql

```
SELECT ProductName, Price
FROM Products
WHERE Price > 50;
```

This will return all products whose price is greater than $50.

Example with Multiple Conditions:

You can combine multiple conditions using AND and OR to create more complex filters.

- AND: Both conditions must be true.
- OR: At least one condition must be true.

Example with AND:

sql

```
SELECT ProductName, Price, AvailabilityStatus
FROM Products
```

51

```
WHERE Price > 20 AND AvailabilityStatus = 'In
Stock';
```

This query returns all products with a price greater than $20 that are available in stock.

Example with OR:

sql

```
SELECT ProductName, Price, AvailabilityStatus
FROM Products
WHERE Price > 20 OR AvailabilityStatus = 'In
Stock';
```

This will return products that either have a price greater than $20 or are in stock.

Real-World Example: Sorting a Product Catalog by Price or Availability

Let's say you are managing an e-commerce website, and you want to display a product catalog to your customers. The products are listed in a table called Products, and it contains the following columns:

- ProductID
- ProductName
- Price

52

- AvailabilityStatus

Your goal is to allow users to sort the catalog based on different criteria, such as price or availability. Here are a few examples of how you might write SQL queries for different sorting and filtering scenarios.

1. Sorting by Price (Lowest to Highest):

If you want to show products sorted by price in ascending order, you can use the ORDER BY clause:

sql

```
SELECT ProductName, Price
FROM Products
ORDER BY Price ASC;
```

2. Sorting by Price (Highest to Lowest):

If you want to show products sorted by price in descending order:

sql

```
SELECT ProductName, Price
FROM Products
ORDER BY Price DESC;
```

3. Filtering and Sorting by Availability and Price:

Suppose you want to show only products that are available in stock, and then sort those products by price from lowest to highest:

sql

```
SELECT ProductName, Price, AvailabilityStatus
FROM Products
WHERE AvailabilityStatus = 'In Stock'
ORDER BY Price ASC;
```

4. Filtering by Availability and Price Range:

You might want to show products that are in stock and have a price between $10 and $50:

sql

```
SELECT ProductName, Price, AvailabilityStatus
FROM Products
WHERE AvailabilityStatus = 'In Stock'
AND Price BETWEEN 10 AND 50;
```

This query filters products that are both in stock and priced between $10 and $50, and it can be helpful for showing a selection of products within a certain price range.

5. Filtering and Sorting by Multiple Criteria:

If you want to filter products that are in stock and then sort them first by price (ascending) and then by product name (alphabetically):

sql

```
SELECT ProductName, Price, AvailabilityStatus
FROM Products
WHERE AvailabilityStatus = 'In Stock'
ORDER BY Price ASC, ProductName ASC;
```

This query will show all products that are in stock, sorted by price (low to high). If two products have the same price, they will be sorted alphabetically by name.

Summary

In this chapter, you learned how to use the ORDER BY clause to sort your query results either in ascending or descending order. You also learned how to use the WHERE clause to filter data based on specific conditions, allowing you to target only the data that meets certain criteria. Through real-world examples, you saw how sorting and filtering can be combined to create meaningful queries for an e-commerce product catalog, making it easier for users to find and view products based on availability and price. These skills are foundational for managing and analyzing data in SQL.

CHAPTER 6

WORKING WITH MULTIPLE TABLES

Introduction to Joins (INNER JOIN, LEFT JOIN, RIGHT JOIN)

In SQL, joins are used to combine data from two or more tables based on a related column between them. This allows you to retrieve meaningful data from multiple tables in a single query. There are several types of joins, but the most commonly used are INNER JOIN, LEFT JOIN, and RIGHT JOIN. Each join serves a different purpose and gives different results.

1. INNER JOIN: An INNER JOIN returns only the rows that have matching values in both tables. If there's no match between the tables, those rows are not included in the result.

Syntax:

```sql
sql


SELECT column1, column2
FROM table1
INNER JOIN table2
ON table1.column = table2.column;
```

56

- **Example**: If you want to join the `Customers` table with the `Orders` table based on `CustomerID`, an `INNER JOIN` will return only customers who have placed orders.

2. LEFT JOIN (or LEFT OUTER JOIN): A `LEFT JOIN` returns all the rows from the left table (the first table in the query) and the matching rows from the right table (the second table). If there's no match, the result will include `NULL` values for columns from the right table.

Syntax:

sql

```
SELECT column1, column2
FROM table1
LEFT JOIN table2
ON table1.column = table2.column;
```

- **Example**: A `LEFT JOIN` will return all customers, even those who haven't placed any orders, with `NULL` values for order details.

3. RIGHT JOIN (or RIGHT OUTER JOIN): A `RIGHT JOIN` is similar to the `LEFT JOIN`, but it returns all rows from the right table (the second table in the query) and the matching rows from the left table. If there's no match, the result will include `NULL` values for columns from the left table.

Syntax:

```sql
SELECT column1, column2
FROM table1
RIGHT JOIN table2
ON table1.column = table2.column;
```

- **Example**: A RIGHT JOIN can be used to retrieve all orders, even those that might not have a matching customer (though this is rare in practice).

How to Combine Data from Different Tables

SQL allows you to combine data from multiple tables by using the JOIN operation. Typically, tables are related through a common column (such as CustomerID in both the Customers and Orders tables). The JOIN operation helps you connect these tables and work with data from both tables simultaneously.

To combine data, you will need to:

1. Identify the common column(s) between the tables.
2. Use the appropriate join type (INNER JOIN, LEFT JOIN, etc.) to retrieve the combined data.

58

Real-World Example: Joining a Customers Table with an Orders Table to See Purchase History

Let's consider two tables: `Customers` and `Orders`. The `Customers` table contains details about customers, and the `Orders` table contains details about orders placed by customers. The common column between these two tables is `CustomerID`.

Example Tables:

- **Customers** table:

CustomerID	FirstName	LastName	Email
1	John	Doe	john.doe@example.com
2	Jane	Smith	jane.smith@example.com

- **Orders** table:

OrderID	CustomerID	OrderDate	TotalAmount
101	1	2025-02-15	100.50
102	1	2025-03-10	250.00
103	2	2025-04-05	75.25

In this example, we want to retrieve the customers along with their purchase history (i.e., order details). We will use an INNER JOIN to link the Customers and Orders tables on the CustomerID column.

Step 1: Using INNER JOIN to Combine Data

sql

```
SELECT Customers.FirstName, Customers.LastName,
Orders.OrderID,          Orders.OrderDate,
Orders.TotalAmount
FROM Customers
INNER JOIN Orders ON Customers.CustomerID =
Orders.CustomerID;
```

In this query:

- We are selecting the FirstName, LastName from the Customers table, and the OrderID, OrderDate, and TotalAmount from the Orders table.
- We use the INNER JOIN to match rows from both tables based on the CustomerID column.

Result:

FirstName	LastName	OrderID	OrderDate	TotalAmount
John	Doe	101	2025-02-15	100.50
John	Doe	102	2025-03-10	250.00
Jane	Smith	103	2025-04-05	75.25

The result shows the purchase history of each customer, including their name and order details.

Step 2: Using LEFT JOIN to Include All Customers (Even Those Without Orders)

If you want to show all customers, including those who haven't placed any orders, you can use a LEFT JOIN. This will return all customers, even if they don't have a corresponding entry in the Orders table.

sql

```
SELECT Customers.FirstName, Customers.LastName,
Orders.OrderID,              Orders.OrderDate,
Orders.TotalAmount
FROM Customers
LEFT JOIN Orders ON Customers.CustomerID =
Orders.CustomerID;
```

Result:

FirstName	LastName	OrderID	OrderDate	TotalAmount
John	Doe	101	2025-02-15	100.50
John	Doe	102	2025-03-10	250.00
Jane	Smith	103	2025-04-05	75.25
Bob	Green	NULL	NULL	NULL

In this result:

- John and Jane have their orders listed, as before.
- Bob Green, who has no orders in the `Orders` table, still appears in the result. His order columns show `NULL` because there is no matching data for him in the `Orders` table.

Step 3: Using RIGHT JOIN (Less Common in This Scenario)

Although it's less common to use a `RIGHT JOIN` in this scenario, let's explore what happens if we want to retrieve all orders, including those that might not have a matching customer. A `RIGHT JOIN` can be used, but in most business scenarios, it's unlikely to have orders without customers.

```sql
sql
```

```
SELECT Customers.FirstName, Customers.LastName,
Orders.OrderID,                Orders.OrderDate,
Orders.TotalAmount
FROM Customers
RIGHT JOIN Orders ON Customers.CustomerID =
Orders.CustomerID;
```

Result:

FirstName	LastName	OrderID	OrderDate	TotalAmount
John	Doe	101	2025-02-15	100.50
John	Doe	102	2025-03-10	250.00
Jane	Smith	103	2025-04-05	75.25

In this case, there is no visible difference because every order has a corresponding customer. However, if there were orders without a valid CustomerID, they would still appear with NULL values for customer details.

Summary

In this chapter, you learned how to work with multiple tables in SQL by using JOIN operations. We covered three primary types of joins: INNER JOIN, LEFT JOIN, and RIGHT JOIN. These joins help you combine data from different tables based on related columns. Through a real-world example, we demonstrated how to join a `Customers` table with an `Orders` table to retrieve customer purchase history. Understanding joins is crucial for working with relational databases, as it allows you to pull together relevant data stored in separate tables.

CHAPTER 7

GROUP BY AND AGGREGATION FUNCTIONS

Using GROUP BY for Data Aggregation

The GROUP BY clause in SQL is used to group rows that share a common value in one or more columns. When combined with aggregation functions, it allows you to perform calculations on each group of rows rather than on individual rows. This is particularly useful for summarizing large sets of data.

The basic syntax of the GROUP BY clause is:

sql

```
SELECT            column1,            column2,
AGGREGATE_FUNCTION(column3)
FROM table_name
GROUP BY column1, column2;
```

- column1, column2: The columns that you want to group by.
- AGGREGATE_FUNCTION: A function like SUM(), COUNT(), AVG(), MAX(), or MIN() that performs calculations on the grouped data.

Example:

Let's say you have an `Orders` table that tracks each order made by customers, with the following columns:

- `OrderID`
- `CustomerID`
- `OrderDate`
- `TotalAmount`
- `Region` (the region where the order was placed)

You might want to calculate the total sales for each region. You can use the `GROUP BY` clause to group the data by `Region` and then calculate the sum of `TotalAmount` for each region.

sql

```
SELECT Region, SUM(TotalAmount) AS TotalRevenue
FROM Orders
GROUP BY Region;
```

In this query:

- `SUM(TotalAmount)` calculates the total revenue for each region.
- `GROUP BY Region` groups the results by the `Region` column, ensuring the total revenue is calculated separately for each region.

Aggregation Functions: SUM, COUNT, AVG, MAX, MIN

SQL provides several aggregation functions to perform calculations on a set of values. These functions allow you to summarize data in different ways. Below are the most commonly used aggregation functions:

1. **SUM()**:
   - o Calculates the total sum of a numeric column.
   - o **Example**: Calculate the total revenue from all orders.

sql

```
SELECT SUM(TotalAmount) AS TotalRevenue
FROM Orders;
```

2. **COUNT()**:
   - o Returns the number of rows in a dataset or the number of non-NULL values in a column.
   - o **Example**: Count how many orders were placed by each customer.

sql

```
SELECT    CustomerID,    COUNT(OrderID)    AS
NumberOfOrders
FROM Orders
GROUP BY CustomerID;
```

3. **AVG()**:

  o Calculates the average value of a numeric column.

  o **Example**: Calculate the average order value for each customer.

sql

```
SELECT  CustomerID,  AVG(TotalAmount)  AS
AverageOrderValue
FROM Orders
GROUP BY CustomerID;
```

4. **MAX()**:

  o Returns the maximum value from a column.

  o **Example**: Find the highest order value placed by a customer.

sql

```
SELECT  CustomerID,  MAX(TotalAmount)  AS
MaxOrderValue
FROM Orders
GROUP BY CustomerID;
```

5. **MIN()**:

  o Returns the minimum value from a column.

  o **Example**: Find the lowest order value placed by a customer.

```sql
sql

SELECT    CustomerID,    MIN(TotalAmount)    AS
MinOrderValue
FROM Orders
GROUP BY CustomerID;
```

Real-World Example: Calculating Total Revenue by Region for a Sales Report

Let's assume you are working with an `Orders` table and need to calculate the total revenue generated by each region. This is a common requirement in sales reporting, where businesses want to know how much revenue each region is generating.

Step 1: Structure of the Orders Table

The `Orders` table has the following columns:

- `OrderID`
- `CustomerID`
- `OrderDate`
- `TotalAmount`
- `Region`

Step 2: Query to Calculate Total Revenue by Region

To calculate the total revenue for each region, you can use the `GROUP BY` clause in combination with the `SUM()` aggregation function. This query groups the data by `Region` and calculates the sum of `TotalAmount` for each region.

sql

```
SELECT Region, SUM(TotalAmount) AS TotalRevenue
FROM Orders
GROUP BY Region;
```

Result:

Region	TotalRevenue
North	15000.75
South	20000.60
East	18000.30
West	13000.50

In this result:

- `SUM(TotalAmount)` calculates the total revenue for each region.
- `GROUP BY Region` ensures that the total revenue is calculated separately for each region.

Step 3: Calculate Additional Metrics by Region

You might also want to calculate other metrics, such as the number of orders or the average order value for each region. You can use COUNT() and AVG() to perform these calculations.

Example 1: Number of Orders by Region

sql

```
SELECT Region, COUNT(OrderID) AS NumberOfOrders
FROM Orders
GROUP BY Region;
```

Result:

Region	NumberOfOrders
North	50
South	65
East	60
West	40

Example 2: Average Order Value by Region

sql

```
SELECT        Region,        AVG(TotalAmount)        AS
AverageOrderValue
FROM Orders
GROUP BY Region;
```

Result:

Region	AverageOrderValue
North	300.01
South	307.70
East	300.50
West	325.13

Step 4: Using Multiple Aggregation Functions

You can also combine multiple aggregation functions in a single query to get a comprehensive view of the data.

Example: Calculating Total Revenue, Number of Orders, and Average Order Value by Region

sql

```
SELECT Region,
       SUM(TotalAmount) AS TotalRevenue,
```

```
        COUNT(OrderID) AS NumberOfOrders,
        AVG(TotalAmount) AS AverageOrderValue
FROM Orders
GROUP BY Region;
```

Result:

Region	TotalRevenue	NumberOfOrders	AverageOrderValue
North	15000.75	50	300.01
South	20000.60	65	307.70
East	18000.30	60	300.50
West	13000.50	40	325.13

This result shows:

- The total revenue (SUM(TotalAmount))
- The total number of orders (COUNT(OrderID))
- The average order value (AVG(TotalAmount)) for each region.

Summary

In this chapter, you learned how to use the GROUP BY clause in combination with aggregation functions like SUM(), COUNT(),

`AVG()`, `MAX()`, and `MIN()` to group and calculate data in SQL. These functions allow you to summarize large datasets, such as calculating total revenue, counting orders, or finding the average order value. By applying these techniques, you can generate meaningful reports, such as total sales by region, and analyze trends and performance across different segments of your data. These aggregation functions are key to performing data analysis and reporting in SQL.

CHAPTER 8

SUBQUERIES AND NESTED QUERIES

Writing Subqueries to Return Values Used in Another Query

A subquery, also known as a **nested query**, is a query that is embedded inside another SQL query. It is used to retrieve a value that will be used by the outer query to perform further operations. Subqueries can be used in various parts of a SQL query, including the SELECT, FROM, WHERE, and HAVING clauses.

A **subquery** typically returns a single value (scalar subquery), a set of values (in the case of an IN or EXISTS subquery), or a table (in the case of a FROM subquery). Subqueries are very powerful as they allow for complex data retrieval and filtering in a clean and organized manner.

The basic structure of a subquery is:

```sql

SELECT column1
FROM table_name
WHERE column2 = (SELECT column2 FROM another_table WHERE condition);
```

- **Inner query (subquery)**: The query within the parentheses that retrieves a value.
- **Outer query**: The main query that uses the value returned by the subquery to filter or calculate data.

There are two main types of subqueries:

1. **Scalar Subqueries**: Return a single value.
2. **Table Subqueries**: Return a set of rows.

Types of Subqueries

1. **Subquery in the WHERE Clause**: A subquery in the WHERE clause is used to filter data based on the result of another query.

   Example: If you want to find all orders where the total amount is greater than the average total amount, you can write a subquery in the WHERE clause.

   sql

   ```
   SELECT OrderID, CustomerID, TotalAmount
   FROM Orders
   WHERE TotalAmount > (SELECT
   AVG(TotalAmount) FROM Orders);
   ```

   In this query:

- o The inner query (SELECT AVG(TotalAmount) FROM Orders) calculates the average order value.
- o The outer query retrieves all orders with a TotalAmount greater than the calculated average.

2. **Subquery in the SELECT Clause**: You can also use subqueries in the SELECT clause to return a value alongside the main query's results.

Example: If you want to retrieve a list of customers and the total number of orders they have placed, you can use a subquery in the SELECT clause:

sql

```
SELECT CustomerID,
       (SELECT COUNT(*) FROM Orders WHERE
Orders.CustomerID = Customers.CustomerID)
AS OrderCount
FROM Customers;
```

Here, the subquery (SELECT COUNT(*) FROM Orders WHERE Orders.CustomerID = Customers.CustomerID) counts the number of orders for each customer.

3. **Subquery in the FROM Clause**: A subquery can also appear in the FROM clause, effectively creating a temporary table to be used by the outer query.

Example: Suppose you want to get the average order value by customer, but first, you need to calculate the total and the count of orders per customer:

sql

```
SELECT CustomerID, AVG(TotalAmount) AS
AvgOrderValue
FROM (SELECT CustomerID, TotalAmount FROM
Orders) AS TempOrders
GROUP BY CustomerID;
```

The subquery in the FROM clause creates a temporary table (TempOrders) containing the CustomerID and TotalAmount for each order. The outer query then calculates the average order value for each customer.

Real-World Example: Finding Customers Who Made Purchases Above the Average Value

Let's assume you are working with an Orders table that contains the following columns:

- OrderID

- CustomerID
- OrderDate
- TotalAmount

Goal: You want to find customers who have made purchases above the average order value.

Step 1: Write the Subquery to Find the Average TotalAmount

The first step is to calculate the average `TotalAmount` from all orders. You can write a subquery to get this value.

sql

```sql
SELECT AVG(TotalAmount) FROM Orders;
```

Let's assume the result of this subquery is `150.00`, which means the average order value across all customers is $150.

Step 2: Write the Main Query to Retrieve Orders Above the Average

Now that we know the average order value, we can use this value in a subquery to filter the customers who made orders above the average value.

sql

```sql
SELECT CustomerID, OrderID, TotalAmount
```

```
FROM Orders
WHERE TotalAmount > (SELECT AVG(TotalAmount) FROM
Orders);
```

In this query:

- The inner query (SELECT AVG(TotalAmount) FROM Orders) calculates the average order value.
- The outer query retrieves all OrderID, CustomerID, and TotalAmount values where the TotalAmount is greater than the average.

Result:

CustomerID	OrderID	TotalAmount
1	101	200.50
2	102	250.00
3	105	180.00

This result shows the orders where the TotalAmount is greater than the average value of $150.

Step 3: Improving the Query to Show Only Customers Who Made Multiple High-Value Orders

Let's take it one step further. Suppose you now want to find customers who have placed multiple orders above the average value. You can add a GROUP BY clause and count the number of orders for each customer:

sql

```
SELECT    CustomerID,    COUNT(OrderID)    AS
HighValueOrderCount
FROM Orders
WHERE TotalAmount > (SELECT AVG(TotalAmount) FROM
Orders)
GROUP BY CustomerID
HAVING COUNT(OrderID) > 1;
```

In this query:

- The GROUP BY clause groups the results by CustomerID.
- The HAVING clause filters out customers who have only made one order above the average value. It keeps only those customers who have placed more than one high-value order.

Result:

CustomerID	HighValueOrderCount
1	2

81

CustomerID	HighValueOrderCount
2	3

This shows that Customers 1 and 2 have made more than one order above the average order value.

Summary

In this chapter, you learned how to write subqueries (nested queries) in SQL to return values that are used by the main query. Subqueries can be placed in different parts of a SQL query, including the WHERE, SELECT, and FROM clauses. You also learned how to use subqueries to find customers who made purchases above the average order value, demonstrating how to combine aggregation functions with subqueries to perform complex data retrieval tasks. Subqueries are a powerful tool for filtering, calculating, and analyzing data in SQL.

CHAPTER 9

USING ALIASES AND COLUMN RENAMING

Renaming Tables and Columns Using Aliases (AS)

In SQL, **aliases** are used to give temporary names to tables or columns. This is particularly useful when working with complex queries, making them more readable and manageable. Aliases are temporary, meaning they exist only for the duration of the query. They do not change the actual name of the table or column in the database.

You can create an alias for both tables and columns using the AS keyword. While the AS keyword is optional, it's often used for clarity. Aliases are helpful for improving the readability of your queries, especially when joining multiple tables or performing calculations.

1. Renaming Columns Using Aliases

When you perform calculations or select columns that are derived from other columns, it's often useful to rename those columns with more meaningful names. This is done by using aliases in the SELECT statement.

83

Basic Syntax:

sql

```
SELECT column_name AS alias_name
FROM table_name;
```

- **column_name**: The actual column name.
- **alias_name**: The temporary name you assign to the column for the query.

Example: If you want to show the `TotalAmount` of an order as `OrderValue`, you can use an alias:

sql

```
SELECT TotalAmount AS OrderValue
FROM Orders;
```

This will display the column `TotalAmount` as `OrderValue` in the result set.

2. Renaming Tables Using Aliases

You can also assign an alias to a table, which is particularly useful when you have multiple tables in your query, such as when performing joins. Using aliases for tables helps to shorten long table names and improves readability, especially in complex queries.

84

Basic Syntax:

```sql
SELECT column_name
FROM table_name AS alias_name;
```

Example: Let's say you want to select all employees from a table called `EmployeeDetails`. You can assign an alias to this table like so:

```sql
SELECT E.EmployeeID, E.EmployeeName
FROM EmployeeDetails AS E;
```

In this case, `EmployeeDetails` is aliased as `E`, which simplifies references to this table in the query.

Improving Query Readability with Aliases

Using aliases significantly enhances the clarity and readability of SQL queries, especially when the queries involve multiple tables, complex expressions, or aggregate functions. Aliases provide meaningful names for the output columns and tables, making the query results easier to understand.

For instance, if you're calculating a customer's total purchase value and you want to display it as `TotalPurchases`, you can assign an alias to the result.

sql

```
SELECT    CustomerID,    SUM(TotalAmount)    AS
TotalPurchases
FROM Orders
GROUP BY CustomerID;
```

Here, `SUM(TotalAmount)` is renamed as `TotalPurchases`, making the result clearer to the reader.

Real-World Example: Creating a Clean Report of Employees and Departments with Meaningful Column Names

Suppose you are managing an employee database with two tables:

- **Employees** table:
  - EmployeeID
  - EmployeeName
  - DepartmentID
  - Salary
- **Departments** table:
  - DepartmentID
  - DepartmentName

86

You want to generate a report that shows the employee's name, their department, and their salary, but with meaningful column names. To make the output easier to understand, you'll use aliases for both the column names and the tables.

Step 1: Write the Query to Join the Tables

We will join the `Employees` and `Departments` tables on the `DepartmentID` column and use aliases for the tables and columns:

sql

```
SELECT E.EmployeeName AS Employee,
       D.DepartmentName AS Department,
       E.Salary AS EmployeeSalary
FROM Employees AS E
INNER JOIN Departments AS D
ON E.DepartmentID = D.DepartmentID;
```

Explanation:

- `E` is the alias for the `Employees` table.
- `D` is the alias for the `Departments` table.
- `EmployeeName`, `DepartmentName`, and `Salary` are renamed to `Employee`, `Department`, and `EmployeeSalary` for clarity.

87

- The INNER JOIN combines the two tables based on the matching DepartmentID.

Step 2: Result

Employee	Department	EmployeeSalary
John Doe	Sales	50000
Jane Smith	Marketing	60000
Alice Johnson	IT	75000

The result is a clean and easy-to-read report, where the employee's name, department, and salary are clearly labeled. By using aliases, you make it easy for others (or yourself) to understand the query's intention and the structure of the results.

Additional Example: Using Aliases with Aggregation

Let's expand on the previous example by calculating the average salary for each department and using aliases to rename the columns.

sql

```
SELECT D.DepartmentName AS Department,
       AVG(E.Salary) AS AverageSalary
FROM Employees AS E
```

```
INNER JOIN Departments AS D
ON E.DepartmentID = D.DepartmentID
GROUP BY D.DepartmentName;
```

Result:

Department	AverageSalary
Sales	55000
Marketing	60000
IT	75000

In this query:

- `AVG(E.Salary)` calculates the average salary for each department, and the result is aliased as `AverageSalary` for clarity.
- `DepartmentName` is aliased as `Department` to make the output more readable.

Summary

In this chapter, you learned how to use aliases to rename columns and tables in SQL queries, making the queries more readable and the results more meaningful. Aliases are particularly useful when performing calculations, aggregating data, or working with multiple tables. By renaming columns and tables in your queries, you can create clear, concise, and easy-to-understand reports. This approach enhances the overall clarity of your SQL queries and makes your work more maintainable.

CHAPTER 10

SQL FUNCTIONS AND EXPRESSIONS

Introduction to String, Date, and Mathematical Functions

SQL functions and expressions allow you to manipulate and transform data in various ways to meet your needs. Functions are essential tools that help you process and present data in a more user-friendly format. In this chapter, we'll explore three primary categories of functions: **string functions**, **date functions**, and **mathematical functions**.

1. String Functions:

String functions are used to manipulate text data. These functions allow you to perform operations like concatenation, trimming spaces, and extracting substrings.

- **CONCAT()**: Joins two or more strings together.

   Example:

   ```sql
   SELECT CONCAT(FirstName, ' ', LastName) AS
   FullName FROM Employees;
   ```

91

This concatenates the first and last names to form a full name.

- **UPPER()**: Converts a string to uppercase.

  Example:

  sql

  ```
  SELECT          UPPER(EmployeeName)          AS
  UppercaseName FROM Employees;
  ```

  This converts the EmployeeName to uppercase.

- **LOWER()**: Converts a string to lowercase.

  Example:

  sql

  ```
  SELECT          LOWER(EmployeeName)          AS
  LowercaseName FROM Employees;
  ```

  This converts the EmployeeName to lowercase.

- **TRIM()**: Removes leading and trailing spaces from a string.

  Example:

sql

```
SELECT   TRIM('   '  FROM  EmployeeName)   AS
CleanName FROM Employees;
```

This trims any spaces before or after the EmployeeName.

- **SUBSTRING()**: Extracts a portion of a string.

  Example:

  sql

  ```
  SELECT  SUBSTRING(EmployeeName,  1,  5)  AS
  ShortName FROM Employees;
  ```

  This returns the first 5 characters of EmployeeName.

2. Date Functions:

Date functions allow you to work with date and time values. You can extract specific parts of a date (like the year or month), perform date arithmetic, and format dates for display.

- **NOW()**: Returns the current date and time.

  Example:

  sql

```
SELECT NOW() AS CurrentDateTime;
```

This returns the current date and time.

- **DATE()**: Extracts the date part from a datetime value.

  Example:

  sql

  ```
  SELECT DATE(OrderDate) AS OrderDateOnly
  FROM Orders;
  ```

  This returns only the date part of the OrderDate column (without the time).

- **YEAR(), MONTH(), DAY()**: Extracts the year, month, and day from a date.

  Example:

  sql

  ```
  SELECT YEAR(OrderDate) AS OrderYear,
  MONTH(OrderDate) AS OrderMonth FROM
  Orders;
  ```

  This returns the year and month from the OrderDate.

- **DATEDIFF()**: Returns the difference between two dates.

Example:

sql

```
SELECT DATEDIFF(CURDATE(), OrderDate) AS
DaysSinceOrder FROM Orders;
```

This calculates the number of days between the current date and the OrderDate.

- **DATE_FORMAT()**: Formats a date in a specific format.

  Example:

  sql

  ```
  SELECT DATE_FORMAT(OrderDate, '%M %d, %Y')
  AS FormattedOrderDate FROM Orders;
  ```

  This formats the OrderDate as "Month Day, Year" (e.g., "January 01, 2025").

3. Mathematical Functions:

Mathematical functions allow you to perform calculations on numeric data. These functions are helpful when you need to work with numbers in queries, such as calculating totals, averages, or rounding values.

- **ROUND()**: Rounds a number to a specified number of decimal places.

  Example:

  sql

  ```
  SELECT ROUND(Price, 2) AS RoundedPrice FROM
  Products;
  ```

  This rounds the `Price` to 2 decimal places.

- **FLOOR()**: Returns the largest integer less than or equal to the given number.

  Example:

  sql

  ```
  SELECT FLOOR(Price) AS FloorPrice FROM
  Products;
  ```

  This returns the largest integer less than or equal to `Price`.

- **CEIL()**: Returns the smallest integer greater than or equal to the given number.

  Example:

```sql
sql
```

```sql
SELECT CEIL(Price) AS CeilPrice FROM Products;
```

This returns the smallest integer greater than or equal to `Price`.

- **ABS()**: Returns the absolute value of a number.

Example:

```sql
sql
```

```sql
SELECT ABS(Discount) AS AbsoluteDiscount FROM Products;
```

This returns the absolute value of `Discount`.

How to Manipulate Data in Queries Using Functions

SQL functions can be used in various parts of a query to manipulate data directly within the query itself. Functions can be combined with other SQL clauses like `WHERE`, `ORDER BY`, and `GROUP BY` to refine your query results.

For example, you can use string functions to manipulate column values in the `SELECT` statement, or you can apply date functions in the `WHERE` clause to filter data based on specific date ranges.

Example: If you want to find employees who joined in 2025, you can use the YEAR() function in the WHERE clause:

sql

```
SELECT EmployeeName, HireDate
FROM Employees
WHERE YEAR(HireDate) = 2025;
```

This query selects employees who joined in the year 2025 by extracting the year from the HireDate column.

Real-World Example: Formatting Dates for Display on a User-Friendly Dashboard

Let's say you're building a user-friendly dashboard that displays order information, and you want to format the order dates for display. You can use the DATE_FORMAT() function to ensure that dates are presented in a readable format for users.

Step 1: Retrieve Order Data and Format the Order Date

Suppose you have an Orders table with the following columns:

- OrderID
- OrderDate
- CustomerID
- TotalAmount

To format the OrderDate for display on a dashboard, you might want to display it in a format like "Month Day, Year" (e.g., "January 15, 2025"). You can use the DATE_FORMAT() function for this.

```sql
SELECT OrderID,
       DATE_FORMAT(OrderDate, '%M %d, %Y') AS
FormattedOrderDate,
       CustomerID,
       TotalAmount
FROM Orders;
```

Step 2: Result

OrderID	FormattedOrderDate	CustomerID	TotalAmount
101	January 15, 2025	1	250.50
102	February 25, 2025	2	180.00
103	March 10, 2025	3	320.75

In this result:

- The OrderDate is formatted as "Month Day, Year", making it more readable for users on the dashboard.

Step 3: Filtering Orders from a Specific Date Range

If you want to show only orders placed in 2025, you can combine the `DATE_FORMAT()` function with the `WHERE` clause. For example, to find orders placed in January 2025:

sql

```
SELECT OrderID,
       DATE_FORMAT(OrderDate, '%M %d, %Y') AS
FormattedOrderDate,
       CustomerID,
       TotalAmount
FROM Orders
WHERE DATE_FORMAT(OrderDate, '%Y') = '2025';
```

This query filters the orders to include only those placed in the year 2025, while still displaying the `OrderDate` in a user-friendly format.

Summary

In this chapter, you learned about the different types of SQL functions, including string, date, and mathematical functions, and how to use them to manipulate and format data within your queries. Functions like `CONCAT()`, `DATE_FORMAT()`, and `ROUND()` allow you to transform and present data in more meaningful ways, which is particularly useful when building reports and dashboards. By using SQL functions effectively, you can tailor your query results to meet specific formatting and calculation needs, making the data easier to understand and more user-friendly.

CHAPTER 11

MODIFYING DATA WITH INSERT, UPDATE, AND DELETE

How to Insert New Records into a Database

The INSERT statement in SQL is used to add new rows of data into a table. It's one of the most common operations when interacting with a database, as it allows you to add records for new entries, such as new customers, products, or orders.

Basic Syntax:

sql

```
INSERT   INTO   table_name   (column1,   column2,
column3)
VALUES (value1, value2, value3);
```

- **table_name**: The name of the table where you want to insert data.
- **column1, column2, column3**: The columns in the table that you want to insert data into.
- **value1, value2, value3**: The actual values you want to insert into the columns.

Example:

Let's say you have a `Products` table with the following columns:

- `ProductID`
- `ProductName`
- `Price`
- `Stock`

If you want to add a new product to the catalog, you can use the `INSERT` statement like this:

sql

```
INSERT INTO Products (ProductName, Price, Stock)
VALUES ('Wireless Mouse', 29.99, 150);
```

This query adds a new product, "Wireless Mouse", with a price of $29.99 and a stock of 150 units.

If your table has an `AUTO_INCREMENT` column (like `ProductID`), you don't need to specify a value for that column; it will automatically be generated.

sql

```
INSERT INTO Products (ProductName, Price, Stock)
VALUES ('Bluetooth Speaker', 59.99, 75);
```

Updating Existing Records

The UPDATE statement is used to modify the data in an existing record. You specify the table and set the new values for the columns you want to change. You can use the WHERE clause to specify which records should be updated.

Basic Syntax:

```sql
UPDATE table_name
SET column1 = value1, column2 = value2
WHERE condition;
```

- **column1 = value1, column2 = value2**: The columns and their new values.
- **WHERE condition**: Specifies which record(s) to update. Without the WHERE clause, all records in the table would be updated, so it is important to use it carefully.

Example:

Suppose you want to update the price of a product in the Products table. Let's say you want to update the price of "Wireless Mouse" to $24.99:

```sql
```

```
UPDATE Products
SET Price = 24.99
WHERE ProductName = 'Wireless Mouse';
```

This query updates the price of the product named "Wireless Mouse" to $24.99.

If you want to update multiple columns at once, you can do so by separating each column and value pair with a comma:

sql

```
UPDATE Products
SET Price = 24.99, Stock = 200
WHERE ProductName = 'Wireless Mouse';
```

This will not only update the price but also set the stock to 200 units for the "Wireless Mouse".

Deleting Data Safely

The DELETE statement is used to remove records from a table. It is important to be careful with this statement, especially when using the WHERE clause, as failing to include a WHERE clause will delete all records in the table.

Basic Syntax:

sql

```
DELETE FROM table_name
WHERE condition;
```

- **table_name**: The name of the table from which you want to delete records.
- **WHERE condition**: Specifies which record(s) to delete. If you omit the WHERE clause, all records will be deleted.

Example:

If you want to delete a product from the Products table, such as "Bluetooth Speaker", you would use the following query:

sql

```
DELETE FROM Products
WHERE ProductName = 'Bluetooth Speaker';
```

This query removes the record for the "Bluetooth Speaker" from the Products table.

Important: Always make sure to use a WHERE clause to specify which records you want to delete. Without a WHERE clause, this query will remove **all** records in the table:

sql

```
DELETE FROM Products;
```

This would delete all products in the `Products` table. To avoid this, always double-check your conditions before executing the query.

Real-World Example: Adding New Products to a Catalog or Updating a Customer Address

Let's consider a real-world scenario where you need to manage an e-commerce catalog and update customer information. You may need to add new products, update existing product details, or modify a customer's address.

Step 1: Adding a New Product

Let's say you want to add a new product, a "4K TV", to the `Products` table. The table has the following columns:

- `ProductID`
- `ProductName`
- `Price`
- `Stock`

To add the new product:

sql

```
INSERT INTO Products (ProductName, Price, Stock)
VALUES ('4K TV', 799.99, 50);
```

107

This query adds a new "4K TV" to the product catalog, with a price of $799.99 and 50 units in stock.

Step 2: Updating an Existing Product

If you later want to update the stock of the "4K TV" after a new shipment arrives, you can use the UPDATE statement:

sql

```
UPDATE Products
SET Stock = 100
WHERE ProductName = '4K TV';
```

This query updates the stock of the "4K TV" to 100 units.

Step 3: Updating a Customer's Address

Now, let's say you need to update the address for a customer in the Customers table. The Customers table has the following columns:

- CustomerID
- FirstName
- LastName
- Address

To update the address of customer "John Doe" with CustomerID = 1:

sql

```
UPDATE Customers
SET Address = '123 New Street, Cityville, NY'
WHERE CustomerID = 1;
```

This query updates the address for the customer with CustomerID = 1 to the new address.

Step 4: Deleting a Product from the Catalog

If a product needs to be removed from the catalog, for example, an old "LED TV", you can delete it from the Products table:

sql

```
DELETE FROM Products
WHERE ProductName = 'LED TV';
```

This query deletes the "LED TV" from the catalog.

Summary

In this chapter, you learned how to modify data in SQL using the INSERT, UPDATE, and DELETE statements. The INSERT statement allows you to add new records to a table, the UPDATE statement lets you modify existing records, and the DELETE statement removes records from the table. We also covered real-world examples, such as adding new products to an e-commerce catalog, updating product information, and modifying customer addresses. It is important to use these statements carefully, especially when working with DELETE, to ensure that only the intended records are affected. These fundamental SQL operations are crucial for managing and maintaining your database.

CHAPTER 12

DATA CONSTRAINTS AND INTEGRITY

Defining Primary Keys, Foreign Keys, and Unique Constraints

In relational databases, **constraints** are used to enforce rules on the data. Constraints help ensure that the data remains accurate, consistent, and reliable across the database. In this chapter, we'll cover some of the most commonly used constraints: **Primary Keys**, **Foreign Keys**, and **Unique Constraints**.

1. Primary Key Constraint:

A **Primary Key** is a field (or a combination of fields) in a table that uniquely identifies each record in that table. No two rows in the table can have the same primary key value. Additionally, the values of a primary key cannot be NULL.

- **Characteristics of a Primary Key**:
    - Uniqueness: Each record must have a unique value for the primary key.
    - Non-NULL: Every record must have a value for the primary key (it cannot be NULL).

Example:

111

Let's say you have a `Users` table, and you want to ensure that each user has a unique identifier. The `UserID` column can be defined as a **Primary Key**:

sql

```
CREATE TABLE Users (
    UserID INT PRIMARY KEY,
    UserName VARCHAR(100),
    Email VARCHAR(100)
);
```

Here, `UserID` is the primary key that ensures each user has a unique identifier.

2. Foreign Key Constraint:

A **Foreign Key** is a column (or a set of columns) in a table that creates a relationship between two tables. It points to the primary key in another table. The purpose of a foreign key is to maintain referential integrity between the two tables.

- **Characteristics of a Foreign Key**:
    - It must reference a valid primary key in another table.
    - It can accept `NULL` values unless otherwise defined.

Example:

Consider two tables: Orders and Customers. The Orders table has a CustomerID column that references the CustomerID in the Customers table. This relationship is maintained using a **Foreign Key**:

sql

```sql
CREATE TABLE Customers (
    CustomerID INT PRIMARY KEY,
    CustomerName VARCHAR(100)
);

CREATE TABLE Orders (
    OrderID INT PRIMARY KEY,
    CustomerID INT,
    OrderDate DATE,
    TotalAmount DECIMAL(10, 2),
    FOREIGN KEY (CustomerID) REFERENCES
Customers(CustomerID)
);
```

In this example:

- CustomerID in the Orders table is a foreign key that references CustomerID in the Customers table.
- This ensures that every order must be associated with an existing customer.

3. Unique Constraint:

A **Unique Constraint** ensures that all values in a column (or a set of columns) are unique across the table. Unlike the primary key, a column with a unique constraint can have NULL values (in most database systems), but all non-NULL values must be unique.

Example:

If you want to ensure that no two users have the same email address in the Users table, you can apply a **Unique Constraint** to the Email column:

sql

```sql
CREATE TABLE Users (
    UserID INT PRIMARY KEY,
    UserName VARCHAR(100),
    Email VARCHAR(100) UNIQUE
);
```

In this example, the Email column is unique, which means no two users can have the same email address. However, if NULL values are allowed, multiple rows can have a NULL email.

Enforcing Data Integrity with Constraints

Data integrity is crucial for maintaining the accuracy and reliability of the data in a database. By using constraints, you can

114

enforce rules on the data, preventing invalid or inconsistent data from being inserted into the database.

- **Primary Key Constraint** ensures that each record is uniquely identifiable, preventing duplicate records.
- **Foreign Key Constraint** ensures that relationships between tables are consistent, preventing orphaned records (i.e., records that reference non-existing data).
- **Unique Constraint** ensures that values in specified columns are distinct, preventing duplicate data entries.

These constraints help maintain the **integrity** of the database by ensuring that only valid data is allowed in the tables.

Real-World Example: Preventing Duplicate Email Addresses in a User Database

Consider a real-world scenario where you are building a user database for an application. One of the most important aspects of the user registration process is to ensure that each user has a unique email address. This helps prevent issues like duplicate accounts and ensures that users can log in or receive notifications without confusion.

Step 1: Create the Users Table with a Unique Constraint on the Email Column

To prevent duplicate email addresses, you can define a **Unique Constraint** on the `Email` column. This ensures that no two users can register with the same email address.

sql

```
CREATE TABLE Users (
    UserID INT PRIMARY KEY,
    UserName VARCHAR(100),
    Email VARCHAR(100) UNIQUE
);
```

- The `Email` column is defined with the `UNIQUE` constraint, meaning the database will reject any attempt to insert a duplicate email address.

Step 2: Insert New Users

When a new user registers, you insert their details into the `Users` table. The database will check that the email address is unique before allowing the insertion.

sql

```
INSERT INTO Users (UserID, UserName, Email)
VALUES (1, 'John Doe', 'john.doe@example.com');
```

If you attempt to insert another user with the same email address:

sql

```
INSERT INTO Users (UserID, UserName, Email)
VALUES          (2,          'Jane          Smith',
'john.doe@example.com');
```

The database will return an error similar to the following:

vbnet

```
ERROR: duplicate key value violates unique
constraint "users_email_key"
DETAIL:    Key    (email)=(john.doe@example.com)
already exists.
```

This ensures that the email address john.doe@example.com can only be associated with one user in the database.

Step 3: Updating User Email (Optional)

If a user needs to update their email address, the database ensures that the new email address is also unique. You can update the email address using the UPDATE statement:

sql

```
UPDATE Users
SET Email = 'john.doe@newdomain.com'
WHERE UserID = 1;
```

117

Step 4: Deleting a User

If a user decides to delete their account, you can safely remove their record from the Users table, ensuring that the database does not leave any orphaned records (i.e., data that references a deleted user).

sql

```
DELETE FROM Users
WHERE UserID = 1;
```

Summary

In this chapter, you learned about the importance of data constraints in maintaining the integrity of your database. We covered how to define **Primary Keys**, **Foreign Keys**, and **Unique Constraints**, and how each of these constraints helps to ensure that your data is consistent and reliable. Through a real-world example, we demonstrated how to prevent duplicate email addresses in a user registration system, showing how the **Unique Constraint** can enforce data integrity by rejecting duplicate data. By properly applying these constraints, you can ensure that your database maintains accurate and consistent data.

CHAPTER 13

TRANSACTIONS AND TRANSACTION CONTROL

Introduction to Transactions and ACID Properties

A **transaction** in SQL is a sequence of one or more SQL operations that are executed as a single unit. These operations are treated as a single "transaction" because they must either all succeed or all fail. Transactions are essential for ensuring that a database remains consistent, even in the event of errors, power failures, or other interruptions.

ACID Properties: The **ACID** properties guarantee that database transactions are processed reliably and ensure the integrity of the database. ACID stands for:

- **Atomicity**: This property ensures that all the operations within a transaction are completed. If any part of the transaction fails, the entire transaction is rolled back, and no changes are made to the database.

  Example: If you are transferring money from one account to another, both the debit and the credit must happen together. If one fails, neither should happen.

119

- **Consistency**: The database must transition from one valid state to another. The integrity of the database is maintained before and after the transaction.

  Example: If you add data to a table, the transaction ensures that the data added is consistent with the rules of the database (e.g., no invalid or duplicate data).

- **Isolation**: Transactions are isolated from each other. One transaction's changes are not visible to other transactions until the transaction is complete. This prevents conflicts when multiple transactions are happening at the same time.

  Example: If two people try to withdraw money from the same account at the same time, each transaction should be isolated so that no transaction sees the intermediate states of another.

- **Durability**: Once a transaction is committed, its changes are permanent, even if there is a system crash or failure.

  Example: After completing a transaction, the changes are saved to the database, and they will not be lost, even if the system crashes immediately afterward.

COMMIT, ROLLBACK, and SAVEPOINT

SQL provides several commands to manage transactions and control the changes made during a transaction. These are **COMMIT**, **ROLLBACK**, and **SAVEPOINT**.

1. COMMIT: The `COMMIT` statement is used to save all the changes made during the current transaction to the database. Once you issue a `COMMIT`, the changes are permanent and cannot be undone.

Syntax:

```sql
COMMIT;
```

Example: If you are transferring money from one account to another, you would commit the transaction after both the debit and credit operations are completed:

```sql
BEGIN;

UPDATE Accounts
SET Balance = Balance - 100
WHERE AccountID = 1;
```

```
UPDATE Accounts
SET Balance = Balance + 100
WHERE AccountID = 2;

COMMIT;
```

In this example:

- The transaction begins with BEGIN.
- The balance is updated in both accounts.
- The changes are saved to the database with COMMIT.

2. ROLLBACK: The ROLLBACK statement is used to undo all the changes made during the current transaction. If an error occurs or a condition is not met during a transaction, you can use ROLLBACK to revert all changes made by that transaction, ensuring the database remains consistent.

Syntax:

sql

```
ROLLBACK;
```

Example: If there is an issue while processing the payment or updating the records, you can use ROLLBACK to undo all changes:

sql

```
BEGIN;


UPDATE Accounts
SET Balance = Balance - 100
WHERE AccountID = 1;


-- Simulate an error
ROLLBACK;
```

In this example:

- The transaction begins with BEGIN.
- The debit operation is executed.
- ROLLBACK undoes the change, ensuring the balance in Account 1 is not modified.

3. SAVEPOINT: The SAVEPOINT command allows you to set a point within a transaction to which you can later roll back. This is useful if you want to rollback part of the transaction rather than the entire transaction.

Syntax:

```
sql


SAVEPOINT savepoint_name;
```

Example: You may want to perform several updates in a transaction, but you only want to rollback to a certain point if something goes wrong, rather than rolling back the entire transaction.

```sql

BEGIN;

UPDATE Accounts
SET Balance = Balance - 100
WHERE AccountID = 1;

SAVEPOINT point1;

UPDATE Accounts
SET Balance = Balance + 100
WHERE AccountID = 2;

-- Simulate an error after saving a point
ROLLBACK TO point1;

COMMIT;
```

In this example:

- A SAVEPOINT named point1 is created after updating the balance of Account 1.
- If something goes wrong in the second UPDATE statement (e.g., updating Account 2), the transaction can be rolled back to the savepoint point1, so only the changes related

to Account 1 are undone, and the rest of the transaction is retained.

Real-World Example: Ensuring Consistency When Processing a Customer's Order Payment

In a real-world scenario, when processing a customer's payment, you want to ensure that the payment is deducted from the customer's account and credited to the merchant's account, and you want to do this as a single transaction. If anything goes wrong, you should be able to roll back all changes to ensure data consistency.

Step 1: Begin the Transaction

Start by beginning a transaction to group all operations.

sql

```
BEGIN;
```

Step 2: Deduct Payment from Customer Account

Assume the customer's account is `AccountID` = 1, and the payment is $100.

sql

```
UPDATE Accounts
```

125

```
SET Balance = Balance - 100
WHERE AccountID = 1;
```

Step 3: Credit the Merchant's Account

Now, credit the payment amount to the merchant's account, `AccountID = 2`.

sql

```
UPDATE Accounts
SET Balance = Balance + 100
WHERE AccountID = 2;
```

Step 4: Check for Errors

At this point, if you detect an error (e.g., the customer doesn't have enough balance or there's a problem processing the payment), you can use `ROLLBACK` to undo the transaction.

sql

```
-- Simulate an error
ROLLBACK;
```

Step 5: Commit the Transaction

If both updates are successful and no errors are encountered, commit the transaction to make the changes permanent.

```
sql
```

```
COMMIT;
```

In this example:

- The transaction begins with BEGIN.
- The payment is deducted from the customer's account, and the amount is added to the merchant's account.
- If anything goes wrong (e.g., insufficient funds), ROLLBACK is used to undo the changes.
- If everything is successful, COMMIT is used to save the changes.

Summary

In this chapter, you learned about **transactions** and how they are used to ensure that a series of database operations are executed as a single unit. You also explored the **ACID** properties that guarantee the reliability of transactions, including **Atomicity**, **Consistency**, **Isolation**, and **Durability**. We covered key SQL commands such as COMMIT, ROLLBACK, and SAVEPOINT, which are used to manage transactions and ensure that changes to the database are either fully applied or fully rolled back. Through a real-world example of processing a customer's order payment, you saw how transactions can maintain consistency and prevent data corruption in case of errors.

127

CHAPTER 14

INDEXING FOR PERFORMANCE OPTIMIZATION

Understanding How Indexes Work

An **index** in a database is a data structure that improves the speed of data retrieval operations. It is similar to an index in a book, where you can quickly locate a topic by looking it up in the index rather than scanning the entire book. In a database, indexes help to speed up query processing by allowing the database management system (DBMS) to find rows more quickly.

Indexes are created on columns that are frequently searched, sorted, or joined. When a query includes conditions such as WHERE, ORDER BY, or JOIN, the database engine can use the index to locate the relevant rows much faster than it could by scanning the entire table.

How Indexes Work:

1. **Search Optimization**: Without an index, the database performs a full table scan, checking every row in the table. With an index, the database can quickly locate the data by searching through the index structure, which is typically much smaller and more efficient than the full table.

2. **Types of Indexes**:

   o **Single-Column Index**: An index created on a single column.

   o **Composite Index**: An index created on multiple columns.

3. **B-Tree Index**: Most databases use B-tree indexing (a type of balanced tree structure) to store and organize index data. It allows for efficient searching, insertion, and deletion of data.

4. **Hash Index**: A hash index uses a hash function to map the values in a column to a fixed-size array. This is useful for equality searches (i.e., =), but less efficient for range queries.

Creating Indexes for Faster Queries

You can create an index on a table column using the CREATE INDEX statement. This improves query performance by allowing the DBMS to use the index to quickly locate the rows that match the query conditions.

Basic Syntax to Create an Index:

sql

```
CREATE INDEX index_name
ON table_name (column1, column2, ...);
```

- `index_name`: The name of the index.
- `table_name`: The name of the table where the index will be created.
- `column1`, `column2`, `...`: The columns that will be indexed.

Example:

If you have a `Products` table and you frequently search for products by `ProductName`, you can create an index on the `ProductName` column:

sql

```
CREATE INDEX idx_product_name
ON Products (ProductName);
```

This index will help speed up queries that search for products by name, such as:

sql

```
SELECT * FROM Products WHERE ProductName = 'Wireless Mouse';
```

The index allows the database to locate the "Wireless Mouse" record much faster than scanning all rows in the `Products` table.

Creating Composite Index:

If you frequently query multiple columns together, you can create a **composite index** on multiple columns. For example, if you often search for products by both Category and Price, you can create a composite index:

sql

```
CREATE INDEX idx_category_price
ON Products (Category, Price);
```

This index improves queries like:

sql

```
SELECT * FROM Products WHERE Category =
'Electronics' AND Price > 100;
```

The composite index allows the database to efficiently filter results based on both Category and Price simultaneously.

Real-World Example: Speeding Up Search Queries in an Online Store Database

Let's consider an online store that has a Products table with the following columns:

- ProductID (Primary Key)
- ProductName
- Category

- Price
- Stock
- Description

As the store grows, users may frequently search for products by `ProductName` or `Category`, and the database performance can suffer if there are too many rows. To speed up these queries, you can create indexes on the columns that are most frequently used in search queries.

Step 1: Index on ProductName

If customers often search for products by name, an index on the `ProductName` column will speed up searches. For example, when a user searches for "Wireless Mouse," an index will help the database find the product faster.

sql

```
CREATE INDEX idx_product_name
ON Products (ProductName);
```

Step 2: Index on Category and Price

If customers frequently filter products by category or price range, a composite index on `Category` and `Price` can significantly improve performance. For instance, customers might search for "Electronics" in the price range of $100 to $500.

```sql
```

```sql
CREATE INDEX idx_category_price
ON Products (Category, Price);
```

This index optimizes queries such as:

```sql
```

```sql
SELECT * FROM Products WHERE Category =
'Electronics' AND Price BETWEEN 100 AND 500;
```

Step 3: Index on Stock for Popular Products

If you want to make it easy to find products that are in stock or out of stock, you can create an index on the `Stock` column. This is particularly useful for queries like:

```sql
```

```sql
SELECT * FROM Products WHERE Stock > 0;
```

Creating an index on `Stock` speeds up searches for available products:

```sql
```

```sql
CREATE INDEX idx_stock
ON Products (Stock);
```

Step 4: Query Performance Comparison

Without indexes, a query like:

sql

```
SELECT * FROM Products WHERE ProductName = 'Wireless Mouse';
```

Requires the database to scan the entire table, row by row, to find matches. This can be very slow when there are millions of products in the database.

However, after creating the `idx_product_name` index, the database can quickly find the "Wireless Mouse" using the index, which is much faster than scanning the entire table.

Maintaining Indexes

Indexes can improve query performance, but they also come with some costs:

1. **Storage**: Indexes take up additional disk space.
2. **Insert/Update/Delete Performance**: Indexes slow down insert, update, and delete operations because the index also needs to be updated when data is modified.

To maintain performance, it's important to periodically evaluate the usage of indexes and remove any unnecessary indexes. If you no longer use an index, you can drop it with the following command:

sql

```
DROP INDEX index_name;
```

Example:

sql

```
DROP INDEX idx_product_name;
```

Summary

In this chapter, you learned how **indexes** improve query performance by allowing the database to quickly locate data without scanning entire tables. You also learned how to create indexes on individual columns or multiple columns (composite indexes) to optimize searches and queries. By applying these techniques, you can speed up search queries in an online store database and improve overall performance. However, it is important to balance the use of indexes with their impact on storage and data modification operations. Properly optimizing and managing indexes is a key part of maintaining a high-performance database.

CHAPTER 15

VIEWS AND VIRTUAL TABLES

Using Views to Create Reusable Query Results

A **view** in SQL is essentially a virtual table. It is defined by a SQL query that retrieves data from one or more tables. The data in a view is not stored separately; instead, it is dynamically generated each time the view is queried. Views provide a way to encapsulate complex queries and present data in a simplified or customized manner, making it easier for users or applications to work with.

Basic Syntax for Creating a View:

```sql
CREATE VIEW view_name AS
SELECT column1, column2
FROM table_name
WHERE condition;
```

- `view_name`: The name of the view you want to create.
- `SELECT`: The query that defines the data to be displayed in the view.

Example:

Let's say you want to create a view that shows the list of products with their category names, but without showing sensitive or unnecessary data like `CostPrice`. You can create a view like this:

sql

```
CREATE VIEW ProductDetails AS
SELECT ProductName, Category, Price
FROM Products;
```

In this example, the `ProductDetails` view contains the `ProductName`, `Category`, and `Price` of products, but it excludes any unnecessary columns. Whenever you query `ProductDetails`, it returns the results of the underlying `SELECT` query.

Benefits and Limitations of Views

Benefits:

1. **Simplifies Complex Queries**: Views can encapsulate complex queries and allow users to query a simple, reusable virtual table. This is especially helpful for queries that involve multiple joins or aggregations.

Example: Instead of writing the same complex query to get customer order details, you can create a view that simplifies the process.

2. **Data Security**: Views allow you to expose only certain columns or rows of the data to users. For instance, you can create a view that excludes sensitive columns like `Salary` from an employee table, while still allowing access to other non-sensitive data.

3. **Reusability**: Once created, views can be reused in multiple queries, which can save time and effort. They can serve as predefined templates for common queries that users often run.

4. **Abstraction**: Views provide a level of abstraction over the underlying database schema. Users can interact with the view without needing to understand the structure of the base tables or complex joins.

Limitations:

1. **Performance Impact**: Views can slow down query performance because they do not store data. Every time the view is queried, the underlying query must be executed. If the view is based on a complex query, it can lead to performance issues, especially with large datasets.

2. **No Indexes**: You cannot create indexes on views directly. Although indexes can be created on the underlying tables,

this limitation means that views cannot benefit from indexing to speed up query performance.

3. **Cannot Be Indexed**: While you can index the base tables, views themselves do not allow indexing, which can affect the performance of queries that depend on them.

4. **Read-Only**: Some views are read-only, especially when they involve complex queries like joins or aggregations. If a view is based on multiple tables, modifying the data through the view may not be possible unless the view is simple and refers to a single table.

Real-World Example: Creating a View to Display User Statistics Without Modifying the Base Data

Let's say you have a `Users` table with the following columns:

- `UserID`
- `UserName`
- `SignupDate`
- `LastLogin`
- `TotalPurchases`

You want to generate a report showing user statistics, such as the number of users who signed up in the last 30 days, without modifying the base `Users` table itself.

Step 1: Creating a View for User Statistics

You can create a view that calculates the number of days since the user's last login, so that when you query the view, it provides a report of active users and their statistics.

sql

```
CREATE VIEW UserStatistics AS
SELECT UserID,
       UserName,
       DATEDIFF(CURDATE(),      LastLogin)      AS
DaysSinceLastLogin,
       TotalPurchases
FROM Users;
```

In this query:

- The DATEDIFF() function calculates the number of days since the user's last login.
- The UserStatistics view now contains the UserID, UserName, DaysSinceLastLogin, and TotalPurchases.

Step 2: Querying the View to Get User Statistics

Now, you can query the UserStatistics view to retrieve data about users who are most likely active, such as users who logged in within the last 7 days:

sql

```
SELECT  UserID,  UserName,  DaysSinceLastLogin,
TotalPurchases
FROM UserStatistics
WHERE DaysSinceLastLogin <= 7;
```

Result:

UserID	UserName	DaysSinceLastLogin	TotalPurchases
1	John Doe	2	15
3	Jane Smith	3	22
5	Alice Brown	1	5

This result shows all users who have logged in within the last 7 days, along with their total purchases. The view allows you to query this data without modifying the original Users table directly.

Step 3: Additional Queries

You can perform other queries on the UserStatistics view to gather different user insights. For example, you can find users who have made the most purchases:

```
sql
```

```
SELECT UserID, UserName, TotalPurchases
FROM UserStatistics
ORDER BY TotalPurchases DESC;
```

Result:

UserID	UserName	TotalPurchases
2	Bob Marley	50
4	Charlie Brown	40
1	John Doe	15

This query retrieves users sorted by their `TotalPurchases`, displaying the highest purchasers at the top.

Summary

In this chapter, you learned how **views** can be used to simplify queries, provide abstraction, and enhance data security by allowing you to encapsulate complex logic into reusable virtual tables. We also discussed the benefits and limitations of views, such as their ability to improve query readability and enforce security, while also noting the potential performance issues. Through a real-world example, we showed how a view can be used to create a report of user statistics without modifying the underlying data. Views are a powerful tool for organizing and presenting data in a way that is both efficient and easy to manage.

CHAPTER 16

STORED PROCEDURES AND FUNCTIONS

Writing Reusable SQL Code with Stored Procedures and Functions

In SQL, **stored procedures** and **functions** allow you to encapsulate logic in the database and reuse it across multiple queries. They are both types of **programmable objects** in the database, but they differ in their purpose and functionality.

- **Stored Procedures**: A stored procedure is a collection of SQL statements that can be executed together as a single unit. Stored procedures are typically used for tasks like data modification (e.g., inserting, updating, deleting data) or for encapsulating complex business logic that may need to be reused. Stored procedures do not return a value but can modify the database or output information.

- **Functions**: A function is similar to a stored procedure but returns a value. Functions are typically used for computations or calculations, and they can be used in SQL queries as part of the SELECT, WHERE, or HAVING clauses. Unlike stored procedures, functions must return a value.

144

Both stored procedures and functions allow for better **modularity**, **reusability**, and **performance optimization** because you can centralize common operations and reduce the need for redundant code.

How to Create and Execute Stored Procedures

1. Creating a Stored Procedure: The basic syntax to create a stored procedure is:

sql

```
CREATE   PROCEDURE   procedure_name   (parameter1
datatype, parameter2 datatype, ...)
BEGIN
    SQL_statement1;
    SQL_statement2;
    ...
END;
```

- **procedure_name**: The name of the stored procedure.
- **parameters**: Input values that the procedure will use, if any.
- **SQL_statements**: The SQL code that makes up the logic of the procedure.

Example: Let's say you want to create a stored procedure that updates the stock level of a product based on the product ID and the quantity to be added. You can write a procedure as follows:

145

sql

```sql
CREATE PROCEDURE UpdateStock (IN product_id INT,
IN quantity INT)
BEGIN
    UPDATE Products
    SET Stock = Stock + quantity
    WHERE ProductID = product_id;
END;
```

In this example:

- UpdateStock is the name of the stored procedure.
- product_id and quantity are input parameters used to specify which product's stock should be updated and by how much.

2. Executing a Stored Procedure: To execute a stored procedure, use the CALL statement and pass the necessary arguments:

sql

```sql
CALL UpdateStock(1, 50);
```

This executes the UpdateStock procedure, updating the stock of the product with ProductID = 1 by adding 50 units to it.

How to Create and Execute Functions

1. Creating a Function: The syntax for creating a function is similar to that of a stored procedure but includes a RETURN statement, which specifies the value the function will return.

sql

```
CREATE    FUNCTION   function_name    (parameter1
datatype, parameter2 datatype, ...)
RETURNS return_datatype
BEGIN
    SQL_statements;
    RETURN result;
END;
```

- **function_name**: The name of the function.
- **parameters**: Input values that the function will use.
- **RETURN**: The value that the function will return.

Example: Let's say you want to create a function that calculates the total value of a product's stock based on its price and quantity in stock.

sql

```
CREATE     FUNCTION    CalculateTotalStockValue
(product_id INT)
RETURNS DECIMAL(10, 2)
```

```
BEGIN
    DECLARE total_value DECIMAL(10, 2);
    SELECT Price * Stock INTO total_value
    FROM Products
    WHERE ProductID = product_id;
    RETURN total_value;
END;
```

In this example:

- `CalculateTotalStockValue` is the name of the function.
- It takes `product_id` as a parameter and returns a `DECIMAL` value representing the total stock value for that product.
- The function calculates the total value by multiplying the price and stock of the given product.

2. Executing a Function: You can use a function in a query just like any other value:

sql

```
SELECT                                  ProductName,
CalculateTotalStockValue(ProductID)              AS
TotalStockValue
FROM Products;
```

This query uses the `CalculateTotalStockValue` function to calculate and display the total value of each product's stock.

Real-World Example: Automating the Process of Updating Inventory Levels

In an e-commerce system, you might need to update inventory levels every time a customer places an order. This process can be automated using a stored procedure to ensure that the inventory is updated consistently and accurately.

Step 1: Create a Stored Procedure for Updating Inventory

The goal of the stored procedure is to deduct the quantity of a product when an order is placed. The stored procedure can accept `OrderID` and `ProductID` as parameters and update the `Stock` in the `Products` table.

sql

```
CREATE  PROCEDURE  UpdateInventory  (IN  order_id
INT)
BEGIN
    DECLARE product_id INT;
    DECLARE quantity INT;

    -- Get the product details for the order
    DECLARE order_cursor CURSOR FOR
    SELECT ProductID, Quantity
```

```
FROM OrderDetails
WHERE OrderID = order_id;

OPEN order_cursor;

-- Loop through all the products in the order
FETCH NEXT FROM order_cursor INTO product_id,
quantity;

WHILE (FOUND)
DO
    -- Update the stock level for each
product
    UPDATE Products
    SET Stock = Stock - quantity
    WHERE ProductID = product_id;

    FETCH NEXT FROM order_cursor INTO
product_id, quantity;
    END WHILE;

    CLOSE order_cursor;
END;
```

Explanation:

- This stored procedure accepts an `OrderID` and uses a cursor to iterate through the order details to update the inventory for each product.

- For each product in the order, it deducts the purchased quantity from the `Stock` column in the `Products` table.

Step 2: Execute the Stored Procedure After an Order is Placed

Once the order is placed, you can call the stored procedure to automatically update the inventory:

sql

```
CALL UpdateInventory(101);
```

This would update the inventory for the order with `OrderID` = `101` by deducting the appropriate quantities for each product in the order.

Step 3: Checking the Updated Inventory

To check the updated inventory after the procedure has been executed, you can query the `Products` table:

sql

```
SELECT ProductName, Stock
FROM Products
WHERE ProductID = 1;
```

This query will show the updated stock for the product with `ProductID` = `1`.

Summary

In this chapter, you learned how to use **stored procedures** and **functions** in SQL to write reusable code that can simplify complex tasks and automate processes. We covered the syntax for creating and executing stored procedures and functions and explored their uses in real-world scenarios. Using stored procedures to automate processes like updating inventory levels helps reduce errors, improve consistency, and streamline operations. Additionally, functions can be used for calculations and data manipulations that can be reused in various queries. Both stored procedures and functions are powerful tools for improving efficiency and maintainability in SQL databases.

CHAPTER 17

TRIGGERS AND EVENTS

Introduction to Triggers and Their Use Cases

A **trigger** is a special type of stored procedure in SQL that automatically runs (or "fires") when certain events occur in the database. Triggers are associated with a table and are activated by specific changes, such as **INSERT**, **UPDATE**, or **DELETE** operations.

Triggers are useful for maintaining data integrity, automating actions, and implementing business rules without requiring manual intervention. Triggers are typically used to enforce rules that must be applied to data changes, such as automatically updating related records or preventing certain types of changes.

Types of Triggers:

1. **BEFORE Trigger**: Fires before an insert, update, or delete operation is executed. This is useful when you need to validate or modify data before it is saved.

2. **AFTER Trigger**: Fires after an insert, update, or delete operation is executed. This is useful when you need to take action based on the completed data modification, such as updating related tables or sending notifications.

153

3. **INSTEAD OF Trigger**: Used to perform an action in place of the default operation (e.g., instead of inserting a record, you might modify an existing record).

Basic Syntax for Creating a Trigger:

sql

```
CREATE TRIGGER trigger_name
AFTER INSERT ON table_name
FOR EACH ROW
BEGIN
    -- SQL statements
END;
```

- AFTER INSERT: Specifies that the trigger should fire after an INSERT operation.
- FOR EACH ROW: Ensures that the trigger fires for each row affected by the operation.
- Inside the trigger body, you can write the SQL code to execute when the trigger is fired.

Automating Actions Based on Events

Triggers are designed to automate actions that occur based on specific events in the database. These actions can include:

- **Enforcing data integrity**: Automatically updating related records or validating data before it is committed.

- **Auditing changes**: Logging changes to records (e.g., recording who updated a row and when).
- **Sending notifications**: Automatically sending emails or alerts when certain conditions are met (e.g., when an order is shipped).

By using triggers, you can ensure that actions happen automatically in response to certain database changes, which improves efficiency and reduces the likelihood of human error.

Example of Common Trigger Use Cases:

1. **Automatically Updating Inventory**: A trigger could be used to update product stock levels automatically when an order is placed.
2. **Audit Log**: A trigger could be used to record all changes made to sensitive tables, like tracking updates to employee salaries or customer information.
3. **Preventing Invalid Data**: A trigger can prevent an invalid update or insert, such as ensuring that an employee's salary is never set to a negative value.

Real-World Example: Sending a Notification When an Order is Shipped

In an e-commerce system, you might want to send a notification (like an email or alert) whenever an order is shipped. A trigger can be used to automate this process without the need for manual intervention. When an order's status is updated to "Shipped," the trigger will fire, and the system can automatically send a notification to the customer.

Step 1: Define the Order Table

Let's assume you have an `Orders` table with the following columns:

- `OrderID`
- `CustomerID`
- `OrderDate`
- `OrderStatus` (e.g., "Pending", "Shipped", "Delivered")

You want to send a notification whenever an order's `OrderStatus` is updated to "Shipped."

Step 2: Create the Trigger

You can create an **AFTER UPDATE** trigger that fires when the `OrderStatus` changes to "Shipped". The trigger will automatically execute a stored procedure or function to send the notification.

sql

```
CREATE TRIGGER NotifyWhenOrderShipped
AFTER UPDATE ON Orders
FOR EACH ROW
```

```
BEGIN
    -- Check if the order status was updated to
'Shipped'
    IF   NEW.OrderStatus   =   'Shipped'   AND
OLD.OrderStatus != 'Shipped' THEN
        -- Simulate sending a notification
        CALL
SendShippingNotification(NEW.OrderID,
NEW.CustomerID);
    END IF;
END;
```

Explanation:

- The trigger `NotifyWhenOrderShipped` is defined to fire **after** an update on the `Orders` table.

- The `IF` statement checks if the `OrderStatus` was changed to "Shipped" from another status.

- The `SendShippingNotification` stored procedure is called, passing the `OrderID` and `CustomerID` as arguments to send a notification to the customer.

Step 3: Define the Notification Procedure

The `SendShippingNotification` stored procedure can be a simple procedure that would, in a real-world system, send an email or generate an alert. Here's an example of what it could look like in SQL (assuming the database supports sending emails):

157

sql

```sql
CREATE PROCEDURE SendShippingNotification (IN
order_id INT, IN customer_id INT)
BEGIN
    DECLARE customer_email VARCHAR(100);

    -- Get the customer's email address from the
Customers table
    SELECT Email INTO customer_email
    FROM Customers
    WHERE CustomerID = customer_id;

    -- Simulate sending an email (this is just an
example, in a real system, you would use an email
API)
    -- Example: CALL SendEmail(customer_email,
'Your order has been shipped!', 'Your order ' ||
order_id || ' has been shipped.');
    -- For now, we will just display the message
    SELECT CONCAT('Email sent to ',
customer_email, ' about order ', order_id, '
being shipped.');
END;
```

Step 4: Execute the Trigger

Let's say an order with OrderID = 101 is updated to "Shipped":

sql

```
UPDATE Orders
SET OrderStatus = 'Shipped'
WHERE OrderID = 101;
```

Step 5: Result

- When the OrderStatus is updated to "Shipped", the trigger fires, and the SendShippingNotification procedure is executed.
- The procedure retrieves the customer's email and sends them a notification about their order's shipment.

If the procedure were fully implemented, it could send an email or generate an alert in the system. In this case, the trigger would automate the process of notifying the customer without requiring manual intervention.

Summary

In this chapter, you learned about **triggers**, which are used to automatically perform actions in response to specific events like INSERT, UPDATE, or DELETE operations. Triggers allow you to automate tasks, enforce rules, and maintain data consistency without requiring external logic. We discussed how triggers can be used to send notifications, such as alerting customers when their orders are shipped. By using triggers and events, you can significantly enhance the efficiency and functionality of your database-driven applications.

CHAPTER 18

NORMALIZATION AND

DATABASE DESIGN

What is Normalization and Why It Matters

Normalization is the process of organizing the data in a relational database in a way that reduces redundancy and improves data integrity. The goal of normalization is to design a database structure that minimizes the amount of duplicate data and ensures the relationships between tables are logical and consistent.

Without normalization, databases can become inefficient and prone to inconsistencies. For example, if the same piece of information (like a customer's address) is stored in multiple places, there is a higher risk of data anomalies, such as updates to one entry that do not propagate to others, leading to inconsistent information.

Benefits of Normalization:

1. **Reduces Data Redundancy**: By eliminating duplicated data, you can save storage space and maintain data consistency.

2. **Improves Data Integrity**: Normalization ensures that the data is logically structured and eliminates anomalies that could arise from redundancy.

3. **Simplifies Database Maintenance**: With normalized data, it's easier to update, insert, or delete records without worrying about affecting data consistency in multiple places.

4. **Efficient Data Management**: It leads to more efficient queries and data processing because the data structure is simpler and logically organized.

Understanding the Normal Forms (1NF, 2NF, 3NF)

Normalization involves breaking down a database into smaller, well-structured tables that each represent a single entity or concept. These smaller tables follow specific **normal forms** (NF), which are sets of rules that guide how to structure the data.

Here are the first three **normal forms** (1NF, 2NF, 3NF), which are the most commonly used in relational database design:

1. First Normal Form (1NF): Eliminate Duplicate Columns and Ensure Atomicity

A table is in **First Normal Form (1NF)** if it meets the following conditions:

- **Atomicity**: Each column must contain atomic (indivisible) values. This means no multi-valued attributes, like lists or arrays, should exist in a column.
- **Unique Rows**: Each row must be unique, with a primary key that uniquely identifies each record.
- **Consistent Data Types**: Each column must store data of the same type, with no mixing of data types (e.g., a column should store only numbers or only dates, not both).

Example: Let's consider a simple table of Customers:

CustomerID	Name	Address	Phone Numbers
1	John Doe	123 Main St, City	555-1234, 555-5678
2	Jane Smith	456 Oak Rd, Town	555-8765

In this table:

- The Phone Numbers column violates 1NF because it contains multiple values (multiple phone numbers for a single customer).

To bring this table into **1NF**, we split the phone numbers into separate rows:

CustomerID	Name	Address	Phone Number
1	John Doe	123 Main St, City	555-1234
1	John Doe	123 Main St, City	555-5678
2	Jane Smith	456 Oak Rd, Town	555-8765

Now, the table is in **1NF** because each column contains atomic values and there are no multi-valued fields.

2. Second Normal Form (2NF): Remove Partial Dependencies

A table is in **Second Normal Form (2NF)** if:

1. It is already in **1NF**.
2. There are **no partial dependencies**, meaning that each non-key column is fully dependent on the entire primary key, not just part of it.

Example: Consider a table that includes both a StudentID and CourseID as a composite primary key:

StudentID	CourseID	StudentName	Instructor
1	101	John Doe	Prof. A

StudentID	CourseID	StudentName	Instructor
1	102	John Doe	Prof. B
2	101	Jane Smith	Prof. A

In this table:

- The composite key is (StudentID, CourseID).
- StudentName depends only on StudentID, and Instructor depends only on CourseID. Therefore, both StudentName and Instructor are partially dependent on the primary key.

To bring this table into **2NF**, we need to separate the information into two tables:

1. Students table:

StudentID	StudentName
1	John Doe
2	Jane Smith

2. Courses table:

CourseID	Instructor
101	Prof. A
102	Prof. B

3. `Enrollments` table (to associate students with courses):

StudentID	CourseID
1	101
1	102
2	101

Now, the data is in **2NF** because all non-key attributes (`StudentName` and `Instructor`) are fully dependent on the entire primary key of their respective tables.

3. Third Normal Form (3NF): Eliminate Transitive Dependencies

A table is in **Third Normal Form (3NF)** if:

1. It is already in **2NF**.

2. There are **no transitive dependencies**, meaning non-key columns must not depend on other non-key columns.

Example: Let's consider a Customers table:

CustomerID	CustomerName	Address	State	StateTaxRate
1	John Doe	123 Main St	NY	8.25
2	Jane Smith	456 Oak Rd	CA	7.50

In this table:

- StateTaxRate is dependent on State, not directly on CustomerID. This is a **transitive dependency** because StateTaxRate depends on State, and State depends on CustomerID.

To bring this into **3NF**, we create two tables:

1. **Customers** table:

CustomerID	CustomerName	Address	State
1	John Doe	123 Main St	NY

CustomerID	CustomerName	Address	State
2	Jane Smith	456 Oak Rd	CA

2. **States** table:

State	StateTaxRate
NY	8.25
CA	7.50

Now, there are no transitive dependencies, and the data is in **3NF**.

Real-World Example: Designing a Normalized Database for a Library System

Let's design a simple, normalized database for a library system. The database should track books, authors, and members, ensuring that we minimize redundancy while keeping data consistent.

Step 1: Define the Tables

- **Books Table**: This will store information about each book.
    - BookID **(Primary Key)**
    - Title
    - AuthorID **(Foreign Key)**

168

- o Genre
- o PublishedYear
- **Authors Table**: This will store information about authors.
  - o AuthorID (Primary Key)
  - o FirstName
  - o LastName
- **Members Table**: This will store information about library members.
  - o MemberID (Primary Key)
  - o FirstName
  - o LastName
  - o Email
- **Loans Table**: This will store information about book loans.
  - o LoanID (Primary Key)
  - o BookID (Foreign Key)
  - o MemberID (Foreign Key)
  - o LoanDate
  - o ReturnDate

Step 2: Apply Normalization

1. **1NF**: The data is atomic, with no repeating groups or multi-valued attributes. Each column contains a single value.

2. **2NF**: The data is in **2NF** because there are no partial dependencies. For example, `AuthorName` depends on `AuthorID` and not on the whole `BookID`.

3. **3NF**: The data is in **3NF** because there are no transitive dependencies. For instance, `Genre` and `PublishedYear` depend on `BookID`, not on `AuthorID` or `MemberID`.

Summary

In this chapter, you learned about **normalization** and why it is essential for organizing relational databases. By breaking data into smaller, logically organized tables, you can reduce redundancy, improve data integrity, and ensure the database is easy to maintain. We covered the **first**, **second**, and **third normal forms (1NF, 2NF, 3NF)**, and demonstrated how to apply these principles to a real-world example: designing a normalized database for a library system. By following normalization rules, you ensure that your database is both efficient and scalable.

CHAPTER 19

HANDLING NULL VALUES

Understanding NULL and How to Handle It in Queries

In SQL, **NULL** represents the absence of a value or an unknown value. It is not the same as an empty string ("") or zero (0), and it cannot be compared using standard comparison operators like =, !=, >, <, etc.

NULL can appear in any column of a table, and its purpose is to indicate that a piece of data is missing or not applicable. For instance, a customer may not have provided a phone number during registration, or a product might not yet have a release date. In both cases, SQL will store a NULL value.

It is important to understand that NULL is not equal to anything, not even another NULL. Therefore, SQL provides special operators and functions to handle NULL values in queries.

Using IS NULL and IS NOT NULL Operators

To work with NULL values in SQL, you cannot use the standard comparison operators (=, !=, >, <, etc.). Instead, SQL provides the IS NULL and IS NOT NULL operators for detecting NULL values.

- **IS NULL**: Used to check if a column contains a NULL value.
- **IS NOT NULL**: Used to check if a column does not contain a NULL value.

Syntax:

```sql
SELECT column_name
FROM table_name
WHERE column_name IS NULL;
```

Example: If you want to find all customers who have not provided a phone number, you can use the IS NULL operator:

```sql
SELECT CustomerID, CustomerName
FROM Customers
WHERE PhoneNumber IS NULL;
```

This query returns a list of customers who have a NULL value in the PhoneNumber column, indicating that they have not provided a phone number.

Alternatively, to find customers who have provided a phone number (i.e., where PhoneNumber is not NULL), you can use the IS NOT NULL operator:

```
sql
```

```
SELECT CustomerID, CustomerName
FROM Customers
WHERE PhoneNumber IS NOT NULL;
```

This query returns a list of customers who have provided a valid phone number.

Real-World Example: Filtering Out Customers Who Haven't Provided a Phone Number

In a real-world scenario, you may have a customer database where some customers haven't provided their phone numbers. Suppose you have a `Customers` table with the following columns:

- `CustomerID` **(Primary Key)**
- `CustomerName`
- `PhoneNumber`
- `Email`

You want to filter out customers who haven't provided a phone number (i.e., where `PhoneNumber` is `NULL`) and only show those who have provided their phone numbers.

Step 1: Retrieve Customers Who Have Provided a Phone Number

You can write a query to select only customers who have a non-null value in the `PhoneNumber` column:

```sql
SELECT CustomerID, CustomerName, PhoneNumber
FROM Customers
WHERE PhoneNumber IS NOT NULL;
```

Result:

CustomerID	CustomerName	PhoneNumber
1	John Doe	555-1234
2	Jane Smith	555-5678
5	Alice Johnson	555-8765

This query retrieves the customers who have provided a phone number. It uses the IS NOT NULL operator to filter out customers who have a NULL value for `PhoneNumber`.

Step 2: Retrieve Customers Who Have Not Provided a Phone Number

If you want to find customers who have not provided a phone number (i.e., where `PhoneNumber` is NULL), you can modify the query to use IS NULL:

```sql
sql

SELECT CustomerID, CustomerName
FROM Customers
WHERE PhoneNumber IS NULL;
```

Result:

CustomerID	CustomerName
3	Bob Green
4	Emily Clark

This query retrieves customers who have a NULL value for the PhoneNumber column, indicating they haven't provided a phone number.

Handling NULL Values in Calculations and Aggregations

When performing calculations or aggregations, NULL values are often ignored. For instance, if you try to calculate the sum of a column that contains NULL values, those NULL values are excluded from the calculation.

Example: Suppose you have an Orders table with the following columns:

- OrderID
- CustomerID
- OrderTotal

If you want to calculate the total amount of all orders, you can use the SUM() function:

sql

```
SELECT SUM(OrderTotal) AS TotalSales
FROM Orders;
```

However, if some orders have a NULL value for OrderTotal (indicating that the order total is missing), those rows will be excluded from the sum.

Step 1: Counting Non-NULL Values

If you need to count the number of non-NULL values in a column, you can use the COUNT() function. It will only count the rows where the specified column has a non-NULL value.

For example, to count how many customers have provided a phone number:

sql

```
SELECT          COUNT(PhoneNumber)          AS
NumberOfCustomersWithPhone
```

176

```
FROM Customers;
```

This query counts the number of customers who have a non-NULL value in the `PhoneNumber` column.

Step 2: Handling NULL in Aggregations with COALESCE or IFNULL

If you want to treat `NULL` values as zero in an aggregation (for example, in a sum or average), you can use the `COALESCE()` function (or `IFNULL()` in some databases).

The `COALESCE()` function returns the first non-NULL value in a list of values. If the value is `NULL`, you can replace it with a default value, like 0.

Example: To calculate the total sales, treating `NULL` values as 0, you can use `COALESCE()`:

sql

```
SELECT     SUM(COALESCE(OrderTotal,     0))     AS
TotalSales
FROM Orders;
```

In this query:

- `COALESCE(OrderTotal, 0)` ensures that if any `OrderTotal` is `NULL`, it is treated as 0 in the calculation.

177

Summary

In this chapter, you learned how to handle NULL values in SQL using the IS NULL and IS NOT NULL operators. We explored how NULL values can be handled in queries to filter data and perform aggregations. We also saw how to manage calculations involving NULL values using functions like COALESCE or IFNULL to treat NULL as a default value (like 0). Understanding how to handle NULL values is crucial for ensuring accurate data retrieval and performing reliable calculations in a database.

CHAPTER 20

WORKING WITH LARGE DATA SETS

Optimizing Queries for Performance with Large Datasets

When working with large datasets, the performance of SQL queries can significantly impact the overall efficiency of your application. Large datasets often contain millions or even billions of rows, which makes querying, filtering, and aggregating the data slower if not properly optimized. Efficient querying becomes crucial to avoid long processing times and resource exhaustion.

There are several techniques and strategies that can help optimize queries when working with large datasets:

1. **Indexing**: As discussed in previous chapters, creating appropriate indexes on columns that are frequently queried can drastically reduce query execution time. Indexes help the database engine quickly locate the rows of interest without scanning the entire table.

2. **Avoiding SELECT ***: Instead of selecting all columns (SELECT *), specify only the columns you actually need. This reduces the amount of data transferred and processed.

3. **Limiting Data**: When querying large datasets, especially for reports or user interfaces, it's often unnecessary to return all rows. Instead, use techniques like LIMIT and OFFSET to only retrieve a small subset of rows at a time.

4. **Batching**: For operations like inserts, updates, or deletions, processing data in smaller batches rather than a single large operation can reduce memory consumption and prevent timeouts.

5. **Query Optimization**: Ensure that your queries are efficient by using proper joins, filtering, and sorting techniques. Avoid unnecessary subqueries and ensure that the SQL engine can efficiently execute your query plan.

Let's explore the specific strategies in more detail:

1. Using LIMIT and OFFSET

When querying large datasets, you don't always need to retrieve all the data at once. You can use the LIMIT clause to limit the number of rows returned by a query, and the OFFSET clause to skip a certain number of rows. This is especially useful when displaying results in pages, such as in a paginated report or UI.

- **LIMIT**: Limits the number of rows returned by the query.
- **OFFSET**: Skips a specific number of rows before starting to return results.

Basic Syntax:

sql

```
SELECT column1, column2
FROM table_name
LIMIT number_of_rows OFFSET skip_rows;
```

Example: Let's say you have a `Transactions` table with millions of records, and you want to display the results in pages of 100 transactions. You can use `LIMIT` and `OFFSET` to paginate through the data:

sql

```
-- Page 1: Retrieve the first 100 transactions
SELECT * FROM Transactions
ORDER BY TransactionDate DESC
LIMIT 100 OFFSET 0;

-- Page 2: Retrieve the next 100 transactions
SELECT * FROM Transactions
ORDER BY TransactionDate DESC
LIMIT 100 OFFSET 100;

-- Page 3: Retrieve the next 100 transactions
SELECT * FROM Transactions
ORDER BY TransactionDate DESC
LIMIT 100 OFFSET 200;
```

In this example:

- `LIMIT 100` limits the results to 100 rows.
- `OFFSET` specifies the number of rows to skip, enabling pagination.

Performance Considerations: While `LIMIT` and `OFFSET` help with pagination, large offsets can still be slow because the database has to process all rows before the specified offset. To optimize this, consider using indexed columns (such as `TransactionID` or `TransactionDate`) for sorting and pagination.

2. Batching

Batching is a technique where large operations, like inserting or updating large numbers of rows, are broken into smaller chunks. This helps avoid performance bottlenecks and resource exhaustion. Batching ensures that the database is not overwhelmed by large transactions, and it can also reduce the likelihood of timeouts or locking issues.

- For example, when inserting 10,000 records, you can insert them in smaller batches of 500 rows at a time.

Example: Suppose you need to insert 10,000 records into the `Transactions` table. Instead of inserting all 10,000 records in a single query, you can batch the inserts into smaller groups.

sql

```
-- Batch 1: Insert first 500 records
INSERT    INTO    Transactions    (TransactionID,
TransactionDate, Amount)
VALUES (1, '2025-01-01', 100), (2, '2025-01-02',
200), ... ;

-- Batch 2: Insert next 500 records
INSERT    INTO    Transactions    (TransactionID,
TransactionDate, Amount)
VALUES (501, '2025-01-03', 150), (502, '2025-01-
04', 250), ... ;
```

This reduces the burden on the database and speeds up the process by preventing it from having to deal with one massive insert.

3. Querying a Large Database of Transactions for a Financial Report

Let's consider a real-world example where you need to query a large `Transactions` table to generate a financial report for the year. The table contains millions of transaction records, and you need to calculate the total amount of transactions for each customer.

Step 1: Basic Query Without Optimization

A simple query to get the total amount of transactions per customer might look like this:

183

sql

```
SELECT CustomerID, SUM(Amount) AS TotalAmount
FROM Transactions
GROUP BY CustomerID;
```

While this query is simple, it may not be efficient when working with a large number of transactions because it has to scan the entire table.

Step 2: Adding Indexing for Optimization

To optimize this query, create an index on the CustomerID and TransactionDate columns, as these are frequently used for filtering and grouping:

sql

```
CREATE    INDEX    idx_customer_transactions    ON
Transactions (CustomerID, TransactionDate);
```

This index will speed up the query by allowing the database to quickly look up and group transactions by CustomerID.

Step 3: Paginating the Query Results

If the result set is large and you only need to display a subset of the results at a time (e.g., for a dashboard or report), you can use

LIMIT and OFFSET to paginate the query results. For example, to display the first 100 customers:

sql

```
SELECT CustomerID, SUM(Amount) AS TotalAmount
FROM Transactions
GROUP BY CustomerID
ORDER BY TotalAmount DESC
LIMIT 100 OFFSET 0;
```

For the next page, you would increase the OFFSET:

sql

```
SELECT CustomerID, SUM(Amount) AS TotalAmount
FROM Transactions
GROUP BY CustomerID
ORDER BY TotalAmount DESC
LIMIT 100 OFFSET 100;
```

By breaking the query into pages, you reduce the load on both the database and the user interface.

Step 4: Using Batching for Updates or Inserts

Suppose that you need to update records in the Transactions table in batches. Let's say you need to update the status of

185

transactions that have been processed. Instead of updating all records at once, you can process them in batches:

```sql
sql

-- Batch 1: Update first 500 records
UPDATE Transactions
SET Status = 'Processed'
WHERE TransactionID BETWEEN 1 AND 500;

-- Batch 2: Update next 500 records
UPDATE Transactions
SET Status = 'Processed'
WHERE TransactionID BETWEEN 501 AND 1000;
```

Batching like this ensures that your updates are efficient and reduces the load on the database.

Summary

In this chapter, you learned how to optimize queries for performance when working with large datasets. Strategies such as using LIMIT and OFFSET for pagination, implementing batching for large insert and update operations, and leveraging indexes to speed up query execution are key techniques for managing large datasets. By applying these strategies, you can significantly improve query performance and ensure your database operates efficiently, even with millions of rows. In a real-world example, we demonstrated how to query a large database of transactions for a financial report, highlighting the importance of indexing, pagination, and batching to maintain performance in production environments.

CHAPTER 21

OPTIMIZING SQL QUERIES

Writing Efficient Queries for Faster Performance

Writing efficient SQL queries is essential for ensuring that your database performs optimally, especially when working with large datasets. Inefficient queries can result in slow response times, excessive resource usage, and poor user experiences. Optimizing queries can significantly improve database performance, reducing processing time and system load.

The key to optimizing SQL queries is to understand how SQL engines process and execute queries. By leveraging database features and applying best practices, you can write queries that are both efficient and scalable.

Techniques for Optimizing SQL Queries

1. Use Indexing for Faster Data Retrieval

Indexes are a powerful tool for improving the performance of queries. An index allows the database to quickly find and retrieve rows based on specific column values, rather than scanning the entire table.

- **Indexing Strategy**:

o Index columns that are frequently used in WHERE, JOIN, ORDER BY, or GROUP BY clauses.

o Avoid creating too many indexes, as this can slow down INSERT, UPDATE, and DELETE operations.

o Use **composite indexes** when querying multiple columns together frequently.

Example: If you frequently search for products by ProductName and Category, create an index on these columns:

sql

```
CREATE INDEX idx_product_name_category
ON Products (ProductName, Category);
```

2. **Limit the Amount of Data Retrieved**

When working with large datasets, it's important to limit the amount of data retrieved by your queries. Only retrieve the columns and rows that are necessary for the task at hand.

- **Limit Data with SELECT**: Instead of using SELECT *, specify only the columns you need to retrieve.
- **Limit the Number of Rows with LIMIT**: Use the LIMIT clause to restrict the number of rows returned, especially for reporting or user interface purposes.

Example: Instead of retrieving all columns, only select the ones needed:

sql

```
SELECT ProductName, Price, Stock
FROM Products
WHERE Category = 'Electronics';
```

Use LIMIT to restrict the number of rows:

sql

```
SELECT ProductName, Price, Stock
FROM Products
WHERE Category = 'Electronics'
LIMIT 100;
```

3. **Avoid Using Subqueries When Possible**

Subqueries (nested queries) can sometimes lead to poor performance, especially when they are executed repeatedly. In many cases, you can rewrite subqueries as **JOINs**, which are typically more efficient.

- **Avoid correlated subqueries**: Correlated subqueries are often less efficient because they are executed once for each row in the outer query.

- **Use JOINs instead**: JOINs are usually more efficient because they allow the database to use indexes and process data in a single pass.

Example: Instead of using a subquery to find products with a price above the average price, use a JOIN:

sql

```
-- Inefficient subquery approach
SELECT ProductName, Price
FROM Products
WHERE Price > (SELECT AVG(Price) FROM Products);

-- Efficient JOIN approach
SELECT p.ProductName, p.Price
FROM Products p
JOIN (SELECT AVG(Price) AS avg_price FROM
Products) avg
ON p.Price > avg.avg_price;
```

4. **Optimize WHERE Clauses**

Make sure that your WHERE clauses are optimized by filtering data early in the query execution. Avoid using functions or expressions on columns in the WHERE clause, as these can prevent the database from using indexes effectively.

- **Avoid Functions on Indexed Columns**: Using a function (e.g., `UPPER(column)`, `DATE(column)`) in the `WHERE` clause can prevent the database from using indexes on those columns.

- **Use Direct Comparisons**: Instead of using `WHERE YEAR(date_column) = 2025`, use `WHERE date_column BETWEEN '2025-01-01' AND '2025-12-31'` to ensure that indexes on `date_column` are used.

5. **Consider Query Execution Plans**

SQL engines generate **execution plans** to determine how queries are executed. By analyzing the execution plan, you can identify bottlenecks and optimize your queries further.

Most database management systems allow you to view the execution plan with a command like `EXPLAIN`. This helps you see how the SQL engine processes your query and where it spends the most time.

Real-World Example: Speeding Up a Query That Searches for Products in an Online Store

Let's consider an example of an online store database where we want to search for products based on `ProductName` and

Category. The Products table contains millions of rows, and we need to ensure the query is optimized for fast performance.

Step 1: Start with a Simple Query

Here's a simple query that searches for products by ProductName and Category:

sql

```
SELECT ProductName, Price, Stock
FROM Products
WHERE ProductName LIKE '%wireless%' AND Category
= 'Electronics';
```

While this query might work fine for a small dataset, it will be slow on a large table because the LIKE operator with a leading wildcard (%) prevents the use of an index on ProductName. Additionally, if there are no indexes on Category, the query will need to scan the entire table.

Step 2: Add Indexes to Improve Performance

To optimize this query, we can add indexes on the ProductName and Category columns:

sql

```
CREATE    INDEX   idx_product_name    ON    Products
(ProductName);
CREATE INDEX idx_category ON Products (Category);
```

This allows the database engine to use the indexes and speed up the query by quickly filtering products based on `Category` and performing an efficient `LIKE` search for `ProductName`.

Step 3: Modify the Query to Limit Data

Next, we can add the `LIMIT` clause to limit the number of products returned, especially if the user interface only needs to show a subset of results.

sql

```sql
SELECT ProductName, Price, Stock
FROM Products
WHERE ProductName LIKE '%wireless%' AND Category
= 'Electronics'
LIMIT 50;
```

This query will return only the first 50 products that match the search criteria, improving performance for large result sets.

Step 4: Optimize Using Full-Text Indexes (Optional)

If the `ProductName` search needs to support more complex searches (e.g., searching for multiple keywords), you can use **full-**

text indexes instead of LIKE. Full-text indexing is optimized for searching text columns, especially when using multiple keywords.

sql

```
-- Create a full-text index on the ProductName
column
CREATE FULLTEXT INDEX idx_fulltext_product_name
ON Products (ProductName);

-- Use MATCH...AGAINST for full-text searching
SELECT ProductName, Price, Stock
FROM Products
WHERE MATCH(ProductName) AGAINST('wireless' IN
BOOLEAN MODE)
AND Category = 'Electronics'
LIMIT 50;
```

Full-text indexing allows for faster and more efficient searches compared to LIKE, especially when searching large text fields.

Step 5: Analyze the Query Execution Plan

Finally, you can use the EXPLAIN command to view the execution plan and ensure that the query is using the indexes efficiently:

sql

```
EXPLAIN SELECT ProductName, Price, Stock
```

```
FROM Products
WHERE ProductName LIKE '%wireless%' AND Category
= 'Electronics'
LIMIT 50;
```

The execution plan will show you how the database processes the query, including which indexes are being used, how many rows are being scanned, and how long the query takes to execute.

Summary

In this chapter, you learned how to optimize SQL queries for better performance, especially when working with large datasets. Key techniques include:

1. **Using indexes** to speed up data retrieval.
2. **Limiting the amount of data** retrieved using LIMIT and OFFSET.
3. **Avoiding subqueries** and using JOINs when possible.
4. **Optimizing the WHERE clause** to ensure efficient data filtering.
5. **Analyzing query execution plans** to identify bottlenecks and optimize performance.

By applying these techniques, you can ensure that your queries perform efficiently, even when working with large datasets. In the real-world example, we showed how to optimize a query that searches for products in an online store by using indexing, limiting data, and considering full-text indexes for more complex searches.

CHAPTER 22

ADVANCED JOINS AND COMPLEX QUERIES

Working with Complex Joins and Nested Queries

In SQL, **joins** and **nested queries** are essential tools for combining data from multiple tables and performing complex queries. As you progress beyond basic SQL operations, you'll often encounter situations where data resides in multiple tables that need to be joined in order to retrieve meaningful results.

Advanced joins, such as **INNER JOIN, LEFT JOIN, RIGHT JOIN**, and **FULL OUTER JOIN**, along with nested queries (also called **subqueries**), enable you to write sophisticated queries that extract and manipulate data in powerful ways.

1. Advanced Joins

While basic joins connect two tables, advanced joins can involve more than two tables and more complex relationships. Here's a quick refresher on the most common join types:

- **INNER JOIN**: Returns only the rows that have matching values in both tables.

- **LEFT JOIN (LEFT OUTER JOIN)**: Returns all rows from the left table, along with matching rows from the right table. If there is no match, the result will contain NULL for columns from the right table.
- **RIGHT JOIN (RIGHT OUTER JOIN)**: Similar to a LEFT JOIN, but it returns all rows from the right table and matching rows from the left table.
- **FULL OUTER JOIN**: Returns all rows from both tables. If there is no match, NULL values will appear for non-matching rows.

For more complex scenarios, **SELF JOINS** and **CROSS JOINs** may be used:

- **SELF JOIN**: Joins a table with itself.
- **CROSS JOIN**: Returns the Cartesian product of both tables, i.e., every combination of rows from both tables.

2. Nested Queries (Subqueries)

A **nested query** or **subquery** is a query within another query. Subqueries can be used in various parts of an SQL query:

- **WHERE Clause**: To filter data based on results from another query.
- **FROM Clause**: To treat the results of a subquery as a virtual table.

199

- **SELECT Clause**: To compute values or perform calculations.

Subqueries can be **correlated** (where the inner query references values from the outer query) or **uncorrelated** (independent queries).

Real-World Example: Joining Three Tables to Retrieve Customer Order History, Product Details, and Payment Status

Let's work through an example of a complex query that retrieves customer order history, product details, and payment status. Assume we have the following tables in our database:

1. **Customers** table:
   - `CustomerID` (Primary Key)
   - `CustomerName`
   - `Email`
2. **Orders** table:
   - `OrderID` (Primary Key)
   - `CustomerID` (Foreign Key)
   - `OrderDate`
   - `PaymentStatusID`
3. **OrderDetails** table:
   - `OrderDetailID` (Primary Key)
   - `OrderID` (Foreign Key)

- o `ProductID` (Foreign Key)
- o `Quantity`
- o `Price`

4. **Products** table:

- o `ProductID` (Primary Key)
- o `ProductName`
- o `Category`
- o `Price`

5. **PaymentStatus** table:

- o `PaymentStatusID` (Primary Key)
- o `Status` (e.g., "Paid", "Pending", "Failed")

Step 1: Joining the Tables

We need to join the following tables to retrieve the data:

- `Customers` to `Orders` (via `CustomerID`)
- `Orders` to `OrderDetails` (via `OrderID`)
- `OrderDetails` to `Products` (via `ProductID`)
- `Orders` to `PaymentStatus` (via `PaymentStatusID`)

We will use **INNER JOINs** for each relationship.

Query:

```sql

SELECT
```

```
    c.CustomerName,
    c.Email,
    o.OrderID,
    o.OrderDate,
    p.ProductName,
    od.Quantity,
    od.Price,
    ps.Status AS PaymentStatus
FROM
    Customers c
INNER   JOIN   Orders   o   ON   c.CustomerID   =
o.CustomerID
INNER   JOIN   OrderDetails   od   ON   o.OrderID   =
od.OrderID
INNER   JOIN   Products   p   ON   od.ProductID   =
p.ProductID
INNER JOIN PaymentStatus ps ON o.PaymentStatusID
= ps.PaymentStatusID
WHERE
    ps.Status = 'Paid'   -- Example filter: only
show orders that are paid
ORDER BY
    o.OrderDate DESC;
```

Explanation:

- The query retrieves the following data:
  - `CustomerName` and `Email` from the `Customers` table.

- o `OrderID` and `OrderDate` from the `Orders` table.
- o `ProductName`, `Quantity`, and `Price` from the `Products` and `OrderDetails` tables.
- o `PaymentStatus` from the `PaymentStatus` table.
- **INNER JOINs** ensure that only rows with matching values in the relevant columns from the joined tables are included.
- The `WHERE` clause filters the results to show only orders where the `PaymentStatus` is 'Paid'.
- The results are ordered by `OrderDate` in descending order to show the most recent orders first.

Step 2: Using a Nested Query to Filter by Total Order Value

Let's say you want to show only customers whose total order value exceeds $500. You can use a **nested query** (subquery) in the `WHERE` clause to calculate the total value of each order and filter based on that.

Query:

sql

```
SELECT
```

```
    c.CustomerName,

    c.Email,

    o.OrderID,

    o.OrderDate,

    p.ProductName,

    od.Quantity,

    od.Price,

    ps.Status AS PaymentStatus
FROM

    Customers c
INNER  JOIN  Orders  o  ON  c.CustomerID  =
o.CustomerID
INNER  JOIN  OrderDetails  od  ON  o.OrderID  =
od.OrderID
INNER  JOIN  Products  p  ON  od.ProductID  =
p.ProductID
INNER JOIN PaymentStatus ps ON o.PaymentStatusID
= ps.PaymentStatusID
WHERE

    ps.Status = 'Paid'

    AND o.OrderID IN (

        SELECT OrderID

        FROM OrderDetails

        GROUP BY OrderID

        HAVING SUM(Price * Quantity) > 500

    )
ORDER BY

    o.OrderDate DESC;
```

Explanation:

- The subquery (`SELECT OrderID FROM OrderDetails ...`) calculates the total value of each order by multiplying `Price` and `Quantity` for each product in an order.

- The `HAVING` clause filters to only include orders where the total value is greater than 500.

- The outer query then uses the `IN` operator to filter the orders by those that have a total value greater than 500, ensuring the result only includes qualifying orders.

Step 3: Using a LEFT JOIN for Optional Data

If you want to include all orders, even those without a payment status (i.e., unpaid orders), you can use a **LEFT JOIN** instead of an **INNER JOIN**. This ensures that all orders are included, and if the payment status is missing, it will return `NULL` for the `PaymentStatus`.

Query:

```sql
sql


SELECT
    c.CustomerName,
    c.Email,
    o.OrderID,
    o.OrderDate,
    p.ProductName,
```

```
    od.Quantity,
    od.Price,
    ps.Status AS PaymentStatus
FROM
    Customers c
INNER   JOIN   Orders   o   ON   c.CustomerID   =
o.CustomerID
INNER   JOIN   OrderDetails   od   ON   o.OrderID   =
od.OrderID
INNER   JOIN   Products   p   ON   od.ProductID   =
p.ProductID
LEFT JOIN PaymentStatus ps ON o.PaymentStatusID
= ps.PaymentStatusID
ORDER BY
    o.OrderDate DESC;
```

Explanation:

- A LEFT JOIN ensures that all orders are included, even if there is no matching PaymentStatus. If an order has no payment status, the PaymentStatus field will be NULL.

Summary

In this chapter, you learned how to work with complex joins and nested queries in SQL. We explored:

- **Joining multiple tables** using `INNER JOIN` and `LEFT JOIN` to retrieve data from related tables.

- **Using subqueries** in the `WHERE` clause to filter results based on calculations, like the total order value.

- Practical examples, such as retrieving customer order history, product details, and payment status from multiple related tables.

- The power of **nested queries** and **joins** to build sophisticated reports and queries that combine data from multiple sources.

Mastering complex joins and nested queries will allow you to build powerful SQL queries to extract the exact data you need from a relational database.

CHAPTER 23

FULL-TEXT SEARCH AND ADVANCED SEARCH TECHNIQUES

Implementing Full-Text Search in SQL

In SQL, **full-text search** allows you to perform more sophisticated text searching than simple pattern matching with LIKE. It is especially useful when you need to search for words, phrases, or keywords within large text fields (e.g., product descriptions, customer reviews, articles, etc.).

Full-text search can be optimized for speed and accuracy, particularly in large datasets. Most modern relational database management systems (RDBMS), such as MySQL, PostgreSQL, and SQL Server, support full-text search functionality. In this chapter, we'll focus on MySQL's full-text search capabilities, though similar concepts apply in other RDBMS with slight syntax variations.

1. Creating Full-Text Indexes

Before performing a full-text search, you need to create a **full-text index** on the columns that you want to search. Full-text indexes are specially designed to make text search more efficient.

Basic Syntax to Create a Full-Text Index:

sql

```
CREATE FULLTEXT INDEX index_name ON table_name
(column_name);
```

Example:

Assume we have a `Products` table with the following columns:

- `ProductID`
- `ProductName`
- `Description`

If we want to perform full-text searches on the `Description` column, we need to create a full-text index on that column:

sql

```
CREATE FULLTEXT INDEX idx_description ON Products
(Description);
```

This index will optimize searches that use full-text search techniques.

2. Using MATCH AGAINST for Advanced Text Search

Once a full-text index is created, you can use the MATCH and AGAINST keywords in SQL to perform advanced text searches. The MATCH keyword specifies the columns to search, and AGAINST specifies the search term or query.

Basic Syntax:

sql

```
SELECT column1, column2
FROM table_name
WHERE     MATCH     (column_name)     AGAINST
('search_query' IN BOOLEAN MODE);
```

- **MATCH (column_name)**: Specifies the column(s) to search.
- **AGAINST ('search_query' IN BOOLEAN MODE)**: Specifies the text you want to search for. In BOOLEAN MODE, you can use operators like + (must contain), – (must not contain), and * (wildcard search).

Example: Searching for Products by Keywords in Description

Let's say you want to search for products in your store that have the keyword "wireless" in their description.

210

sql

```
SELECT ProductID, ProductName, Description
FROM Products
WHERE MATCH (Description) AGAINST ('wireless' IN
BOOLEAN MODE);
```

This query searches the `Description` column for the word "wireless" and returns all products whose description contains this term.

Example with Multiple Keywords:

You can also search for multiple keywords by providing them in the search query. For example, searching for products that contain both "wireless" and "mouse":

sql

```
SELECT ProductID, ProductName, Description
FROM Products
WHERE MATCH (Description) AGAINST ('+wireless
+mouse' IN BOOLEAN MODE);
```

In this example:

- The + operator before the keywords `wireless` and `mouse` ensures that both terms must appear in the description for the product to be returned.

211

Example with Excluding Words:

You can exclude certain words from the search using the - operator. For example, searching for "wireless" products but excluding products with the word "keyboard":

sql

```
SELECT ProductID, ProductName, Description
FROM Products
WHERE MATCH (Description) AGAINST ('+wireless -
keyboard' IN BOOLEAN MODE);
```

This query will return products that contain "wireless" but do not contain "keyboard" in their description.

Full-Text Search Options in MySQL

MySQL offers two modes for the MATCH AGAINST operation:

1. **Natural Language Mode (default)**: Searches for words in their natural form, where common stopwords (e.g., "the", "is", "on") are ignored.
2. **Boolean Mode**: Allows more control, including the ability to require or exclude certain words, use wildcards, and search for phrases.

By default, MySQL uses **Natural Language Mode**, but you can specify **Boolean Mode** by including `IN BOOLEAN MODE` in the `AGAINST` clause, as shown in the previous examples.

3. Real-World Example: Searching for Products in a Store Using Keywords and Descriptions

Let's consider an online store database where customers want to search for products based on keywords in the product description. The `Products` table contains the following columns:

- `ProductID`
- `ProductName`
- `Description`
- `Category`
- `Price`

The store wants to allow customers to search for products using keywords and return a list of products that match those keywords in the description.

Step 1: Create Full-Text Index on Description Column

First, we need to create a full-text index on the `Description` column to optimize the search:

```sql
```

```
CREATE FULLTEXT INDEX idx_description ON Products
(Description);
```

Step 2: Implement Full-Text Search Using MATCH AGAINST

Now, we can use the MATCH AGAINST statement to search for products based on keywords in the description. Let's say a customer wants to find all products related to "wireless" and "mouse" in the description:

sql

```
SELECT    ProductID,    ProductName,    Description,
Price
FROM Products
WHERE   MATCH   (Description)   AGAINST   ('+wireless
+mouse' IN BOOLEAN MODE)
ORDER BY Price DESC;
```

This query:

- Searches the Description column for products containing both "wireless" and "mouse".
- Orders the results by Price in descending order, showing the most expensive products first.

Step 3: Handling Multiple Keywords and Exclusions

Customers may want to refine their search by excluding certain keywords, like "keyboard". The following query searches for products containing "wireless" and "mouse" but excluding "keyboard":

sql

```
SELECT    ProductID,    ProductName,    Description,
Price
FROM Products
WHERE  MATCH  (Description)  AGAINST  ('+wireless
+mouse -keyboard' IN BOOLEAN MODE)
ORDER BY Price DESC;
```

This query ensures that the search results contain "wireless" and "mouse" but do not contain "keyboard", and it orders the results by price.

Step 4: Searching for Phrases

If a customer wants to search for products that contain a specific phrase, such as "wireless mouse", you can use the " operator to search for the exact phrase:

sql

```
SELECT    ProductID,    ProductName,    Description,
Price
FROM Products
```

```
WHERE MATCH (Description) AGAINST ('"wireless
mouse"' IN BOOLEAN MODE)
ORDER BY Price DESC;
```

This query returns products whose descriptions contain the exact phrase "wireless mouse".

4. Full-Text Search Limitations

While full-text search is powerful, it does have some limitations:

1. **Stopwords**: Common words (e.g., "the", "is", "of") are ignored by default in natural language mode. This may not be ideal in all situations.

2. **Minimum Word Length**: Some RDBMS, like MySQL, have a minimum word length (usually 4 characters) for full-text search. This means that shorter words might not be searchable.

3. **Performance**: Although full-text indexing significantly speeds up searches, it can still be resource-intensive when working with very large datasets. It's important to monitor performance and optimize your queries, indexes, and database schema.

Summary

In this chapter, we explored **full-text search** and how it can be used to efficiently search large text fields in SQL databases. We discussed how to create full-text indexes and use the `MATCH` `AGAINST` operator to search for keywords, phrases, and specific terms in product descriptions. By leveraging full-text search, we can offer more powerful and flexible search capabilities in applications like e-commerce platforms. We also covered techniques like using `IN BOOLEAN MODE` to fine-tune searches with operators like +, -, and *, allowing users to refine and exclude terms as needed. Despite its advantages, full-text search has some limitations, which must be considered when designing your database and search functionality.

CHAPTER 24

SECURITY IN SQL

Protecting SQL Queries from SQL Injection

SQL injection is one of the most common security vulnerabilities in SQL databases. It occurs when an attacker manipulates SQL queries by injecting malicious SQL code into an application's input fields. This can lead to unauthorized access, data manipulation, or even complete control over the database.

How SQL Injection Works: SQL injection typically happens when user input is directly included in SQL queries without proper validation or sanitization. For example, consider the following simple SQL query:

```sql
```

```sql
SELECT * FROM Users WHERE username = 'user_input'
AND password = 'user_password';
```

If the `user_input` is not sanitized, an attacker could input the following:

```sql
```

```sql
' OR 1=1; --
```

This would modify the query to:

```sql
SELECT * FROM Users WHERE username = '' OR 1=1;
--' AND password = 'user_password';
```

The query now always evaluates to true (1=1), potentially giving the attacker unauthorized access to the system.

Preventing SQL Injection:

1. **Never trust user input**: Always validate and sanitize inputs, even if they are coming from trusted sources.
2. **Use parameterized queries** (also called **prepared statements**) to ensure that user input is handled safely.

Using Prepared Statements for Safe Data Input

The most effective way to prevent SQL injection is by using **prepared statements**. Prepared statements separate SQL code from the data being input by the user. The database engine treats user input as data, not as part of the SQL query, which prevents malicious code from being executed.

A **prepared statement** is a feature of many SQL databases, including MySQL, PostgreSQL, and SQL Server. It allows you to define the SQL query once, then bind user input to placeholders in the query.

Benefits of Prepared Statements:

1. **Prevents SQL Injection**: Since user input is treated as data, not executable code, it cannot modify the structure of the query.

2. **Performance**: Prepared statements are usually faster for repeated queries because the database only needs to parse and plan the query once.

3. **Code Clarity**: Prepared statements improve the readability and maintainability of SQL queries.

Syntax for Prepared Statements:

1. **MySQL** (with PDO or MySQLi in PHP):
   o **Placeholders**: Use `?` for parameterized placeholders.

```php
php


// Using PDO in PHP
$stmt = $pdo->prepare("SELECT * FROM Users
WHERE username = ? AND password = ?");
$stmt->execute([$username, $password]);
```

2. **PostgreSQL** (with pg-promise or psql in Node.js):
   o **Placeholders**: Use `$1`, `$2`, etc., for positional placeholders.

```javascript
javascript
```

```javascript
const query = 'SELECT * FROM Users WHERE
username = $1 AND password = $2';
db.query(query, [username, password]);
```

3. **MySQLi in PHP** (for MySQL):

   o **Placeholders**: Use ? for parameterized placeholders.

```php
php
```

```php
// Using MySQLi in PHP
$stmt = $mysqli->prepare("SELECT * FROM
Users WHERE username = ? AND password =
?");
$stmt->bind_param("ss",          $username,
$password); // 'ss' means both parameters
are strings
$stmt->execute();
```

Real-World Example: Securely Handling User Login Credentials in a Website Database

Let's consider an example of a website login system where user credentials (username and password) are stored in a Users table. We want to handle login securely to avoid SQL injection attacks.

Step 1: Database Structure

Assume the `Users` table has the following structure:

- `UserID` (Primary Key)
- `Username`
- `Password` (hashed)

We store passwords as **hashed values** rather than plaintext for security reasons (e.g., using algorithms like SHA-256 or bcrypt).

Step 2: Vulnerable SQL Query

Here's an example of a vulnerable SQL query that directly inserts user input into the SQL statement:

php

```
// Vulnerable code (Not Safe!)
$query = "SELECT * FROM Users WHERE username = '"
. $_POST['username'] . "' AND password = '" .
$_POST['password'] . "'";
$result = mysqli_query($conn, $query);
```

In this example, an attacker could input the following:

- Username: `admin`
- Password: `' OR 1=1; --`

This would make the SQL query:

```sql
SELECT * FROM Users WHERE username = 'admin' AND
password = '' OR 1=1; --';
```

This query would always return true, allowing unauthorized access.

Step 3: Securing the Query with Prepared Statements

To prevent SQL injection, we should use prepared statements. Here's how you can do that securely:

```php
// Secure code using prepared statements
$stmt = $conn->prepare("SELECT * FROM Users WHERE
username = ? AND password = ?");
$stmt->bind_param("ss",        $_POST['username'],
$_POST['password']);
$stmt->execute();
$result = $stmt->get_result();
```

In this version:

- The query uses placeholders (?) for username and password.

- The `bind_param()` function safely binds the user inputs to the placeholders, ensuring they are treated as data and not executable code.
- The query is executed with `execute()`, and the results are fetched using `get_result()`.

Step 4: Hashing Passwords for Better Security

While handling login credentials, it's important not to store plaintext passwords. Instead, you should hash passwords using secure hashing algorithms like bcrypt or Argon2. Here's an example of how to securely handle password storage and verification in PHP using `password_hash()` and `password_verify()`:

1. **Storing the Password** (during user registration or password update):

php

```php
$hashed_password                            =
password_hash($_POST['password'],
PASSWORD_BCRYPT);
$stmt = $conn->prepare("INSERT INTO Users
(username, password) VALUES (?, ?)");
$stmt->bind_param("ss",
$_POST['username'], $hashed_password);
$stmt->execute();
```

2. **Verifying the Password** (during user login):

```php
$stmt = $conn->prepare("SELECT password
FROM Users WHERE username = ?");
$stmt->bind_param("s",
$_POST['username']);
$stmt->execute();
$result = $stmt->get_result();
$row = $result->fetch_assoc();

if (password_verify($_POST['password'],
$row['password'])) {
    // Password is correct, proceed with
login
} else {
    // Invalid password
}
```

The `password_verify()` function compares the user-input password with the hashed password stored in the database, ensuring secure authentication.

Step 5: Using Parameterized Queries with Other RDBMS

In addition to MySQL, other RDBMS like PostgreSQL and SQL Server also support parameterized queries. Here's an example for PostgreSQL (Node.js):

javascript

```
const query = 'SELECT * FROM Users WHERE username
= $1 AND password = $2';
db.query(query, [username, password], (err, res)
=> {
   if (err) {
       console.error('Error   executing   query',
err.stack);
   } else {
       // Process results
   }
});
```

This uses $1 and $2 placeholders for the username and password and safely executes the query with the user inputs.

Summary

In this chapter, we covered **SQL injection** and how to protect your SQL queries from this common vulnerability by using **prepared statements**. We emphasized the importance of validating and sanitizing user inputs and showed how to securely handle user login credentials by hashing passwords and verifying them with secure methods. Using prepared statements ensures that user inputs are treated as data, not executable code, protecting your database from SQL injection attacks. Additionally, we saw how to implement these techniques in real-world scenarios, such as securing login systems on websites. By following these best practices, you can significantly improve the security of your SQL-based applications.

CHAPTER 25

BACKUP AND RECOVERY TECHNIQUES

Understanding Backup Strategies for SQL Databases

Data is one of the most valuable assets in any organization, and maintaining it securely is essential. **Backup** is the process of creating a of data to prevent data loss in case of system failures, corruption, or disasters. **Recovery** refers to the process of restoring the data from these backups when needed.

SQL databases, especially those with critical business data, require robust backup strategies to ensure that data can be recovered quickly and accurately in the event of a failure.

Backup Types and Strategies

There are different types of backups that serve different purposes. The choice of backup strategy depends on the size of the database, the frequency of changes to the data, and the tolerance for downtime.

1. **Full Backups**:

- o A **full backup** captures the entire database at a particular point in time. It includes all the data, schema, and other database objects.
- o **Pros**: Easy to restore because it contains everything needed to recover the database.
- o **Cons**: Time-consuming and requires a lot of storage space, especially for large databases.

Example (MySQL):

```bash
bash

mysqldump -u username -p database_name >
full_backup.sql
```

2. **Incremental Backups**:
    - o An **incremental backup** captures only the changes made to the database since the last backup (whether full or incremental).
    - o **Pros**: Faster and requires less storage because only changed data is backed up.
    - o **Cons**: Restoration can be slower because you need to apply multiple incremental backups in sequence.

Example (MySQL):

- o MySQL does not have a built-in incremental backup feature, but it can be achieved using binary logs or third-party tools.

3. **Differential Backups**:
    - o A **differential backup** captures all changes made since the last full backup. Unlike incremental backups, which only back up changes since the last backup (full or incremental), differential backups include all changes since the last full backup.
    - o **Pros**: Faster than full backups and easier to restore than incremental backups.
    - o **Cons**: Still requires more storage than incremental backups as the backup grows over time.

Example (MySQL):

- o Differential backups are typically implemented through the combination of full backups and binary logs.

4. **Transaction Log Backups**:
    - o **Transaction log backups** are used in databases that support transaction logging (e.g., SQL Server, PostgreSQL). These backups capture the transaction logs that record all changes made to the database.

o **Pros**: Enables point-in-time recovery, ensuring that you can restore the database to any specific moment.

o **Cons**: Requires more frequent backups to capture all changes.

Example (SQL Server):

sql

```
BACKUP LOG database_name TO DISK = 'transaction_log_backup.bak';
```

Backup Scheduling and Automation

Regular backups are essential to ensure that the data is protected from loss. Instead of manually performing backups, they should be scheduled and automated to run at predefined intervals (daily, weekly, monthly).

- **Tools for Scheduling**:
  - o Use **cron jobs** (Linux) or **Task Scheduler** (Windows) to automate backup scripts.
  - o Database management systems (DBMSs) also offer tools for scheduling backups, like **SQL Server Agent** or **MySQL Event Scheduler**.

How to Restore Data from Backups

Restoring data from backups is as crucial as backing it up. In case of data corruption, accidental deletion, or hardware failure, the ability to restore data efficiently and accurately is essential to maintaining business continuity.

The restoration process depends on the type of backup and the DBMS being used. Here are the basic steps for restoring data from different types of backups:

1. **Restoring from a Full Backup**:
    o   If you have a full backup, restoring the entire database is straightforward. You can use the DBMS's restore command to restore the database to the state it was in when the backup was taken.

    Example (MySQL):

    ```bash
    mysql -u username -p database_name < full_backup.sql
    ```

    Example (SQL Server):

    ```sql
    RESTORE DATABASE database_name
    FROM DISK = 'full_backup.bak';
    ```

2. **Restoring from Incremental or Differential Backups**:
   o When restoring from incremental or differential backups, you must first restore the most recent full backup, then apply the incremental or differential backups in sequence to restore the database to the desired point in time.

Example (SQL Server):

sql

```
RESTORE DATABASE database_name
FROM DISK = 'full_backup.bak';

RESTORE LOG database_name
FROM DISK = 'transaction_log_backup.bak';
```

3. **Point-in-Time Recovery**:
   o For databases that support **transaction log backups**, you can restore the database to any point in time by applying transaction logs to the full backup.

Example (SQL Server):

sql

```
RESTORE DATABASE database_name
FROM DISK = 'full_backup.bak'
```

233

```
WITH NORECOVERY;

RESTORE LOG database_name
FROM DISK = 'transaction_log_backup.bak'
WITH STOPAT = '2025-01-01 14:30:00'; --
Specify the recovery time
```

Real-World Example: Scheduling Regular Backups for an E-Commerce Website Database

Let's consider an e-commerce website where we need to ensure that the database containing customer data, orders, and inventory information is backed up regularly.

1. **Database Structure**:
   - The `Customers`, `Orders`, and `Products` tables are part of the e-commerce database.
2. **Backup Strategy**:
   - Perform a **full backup** every Sunday to capture the complete database.
   - Take **incremental backups** every night to capture changes made throughout the week.
   - Schedule **transaction log backups** every hour to ensure the database can be restored to the most recent state.
3. **Backup Process**:
   - **Full Backup** (every Sunday at midnight):

- Use the following cron job (Linux) to automate the full backup:

bash

```
0 0 * * 0 mysqldump -u username -p
database_name                    >
/backup/full_backup_$(date +\%Y-\%m-
\%d).sql
```

o **Incremental Backup** (every night at 2 AM):
  - Create incremental backups using MySQL's binary logs:

bash

```
0 2 * * * mysqldump -u username -p
database_name --single-transaction -
-flush-logs                          >
/backup/incremental_backup_$(date
+\%Y-\%m-\%d).sql
```

o **Transaction Log Backup** (every hour):
  - Use SQL Server's BACKUP LOG for transaction log backups:

sql

235

```
BACKUP LOG database_name TO DISK =
'transaction_log_backup.bak';
```

4. **Restoring Data**:

   o **Restore the full backup** and apply the **incremental backups** and **transaction log backups** in sequence if data is lost or corrupted.

   o Example (MySQL):

   bash

   ```
   mysql -u username -p database_name <
   full_backup_2025-01-01.sql
   mysql -u username -p database_name <
   incremental_backup_2025-01-02.sql
   ```

5. **Automation**:

   o Automate the backup and restore process using scripts and cron jobs (or Task Scheduler on Windows) to ensure backups happen without manual intervention.

Summary

In this chapter, you learned about **backup strategies** for SQL databases and how to effectively protect your data through regular backups. Key points included:

- The different types of backups (full, incremental, differential, and transaction log backups) and their use cases.
- How to schedule regular backups and automate the process using cron jobs or database scheduling tools.
- The importance of **restoring data** from backups and ensuring that data can be recovered in the event of a failure.
- A real-world example of an e-commerce website's backup strategy, including backing up the database regularly and restoring data when necessary.

By implementing a solid backup and recovery strategy, you can ensure that your data is protected, minimizing the risk of data loss and ensuring business continuity.

CHAPTER 26

SQL FOR DATA ANALYSIS AND REPORTING

Using SQL for Data Analysis Tasks

SQL is a powerful tool for data analysis and reporting. With SQL, you can query and manipulate data to generate insights, make data-driven decisions, and produce detailed reports. SQL is especially useful in transforming raw data into meaningful analysis by applying filters, calculations, and aggregations to derive insights from large datasets.

Some of the most common SQL operations used in data analysis include:

- **Aggregation**: Using functions like `SUM()`, `AVG()`, `COUNT()`, `MIN()`, and `MAX()` to calculate totals, averages, and other key metrics.
- **Filtering and Grouping**: Using `WHERE`, `HAVING`, `GROUP BY`, and `ORDER BY` to narrow down data and group it into meaningful categories.
- **Joining Tables**: Combining data from multiple tables to get a comprehensive view of information.

238

- **Subqueries**: Using nested queries to perform calculations or data transformations before finalizing results.

SQL can be used for various types of analysis, including:

- Summarizing data by time periods (e.g., monthly, quarterly, yearly).
- Tracking key performance indicators (KPIs).
- Segmenting data by specific attributes (e.g., product category, customer region).
- Performing trend analysis and comparison over time.

Creating Complex Reports and Visualizations

SQL is primarily used for data manipulation and reporting, but it can be part of a larger data analysis pipeline that includes data visualization tools. While SQL itself doesn't provide built-in visualization tools (like graphs and charts), it is commonly used to prepare data for visualization tools such as Tableau, Power BI, or Excel.

Here's a breakdown of how to create complex reports and integrate them with visualizations:

1. **Aggregating Data for Reporting**: SQL allows you to aggregate data based on specific criteria. This is useful when generating reports that summarize key metrics, such as total sales or customer activity.

239

2. **Using Grouping and Filtering**: The combination of GROUP BY and HAVING clauses allows you to organize data and filter it based on specific conditions, helping to narrow down the results to match the requirements of the report.

3. **Using Subqueries for Complex Calculations**: Subqueries allow you to perform complex calculations or data transformations before combining the results into your final report.

4. **Exporting Data for Visualization**: Once data is aggregated and filtered in SQL, it can be exported to external tools for visualization. For example, you can export query results to CSV files or directly connect your database to visualization tools.

5. **Joining Data Across Multiple Tables**: Complex reports often require data from multiple sources. SQL allows you to join tables efficiently, helping you generate comprehensive reports that provide a holistic view of your business operations.

Real-World Example: Generating Monthly Sales Reports for a Business

Let's assume we are working with an online retail business, and we need to generate a monthly sales report. The database has the following tables:

1. **Orders** table:
   - o OrderID (Primary Key)
   - o OrderDate
   - o CustomerID
   - o TotalAmount

2. **OrderDetails** table:
   - o OrderDetailID (Primary Key)
   - o OrderID (Foreign Key)
   - o ProductID
   - o Quantity
   - o Price

3. **Products** table:
   - o ProductID (Primary Key)
   - o ProductName
   - o Category
   - o Price

4. **Customers** table:
   - o CustomerID (Primary Key)
   - o CustomerName
   - o Email
   - o Region

Our goal is to create a monthly sales report that shows:

- Total sales per month.
- Sales by product category.
- The number of orders per month.
- The total number of products sold.

241

Step 1: Aggregating Sales by Month

We will start by aggregating the total sales for each month. We can use the MONTH() and YEAR() functions to extract the month and year from the OrderDate.

sql

```
SELECT
    YEAR(OrderDate) AS Year,
    MONTH(OrderDate) AS Month,
    SUM(TotalAmount) AS TotalSales,
    COUNT(DISTINCT OrderID) AS NumberOfOrders
FROM Orders
GROUP BY YEAR(OrderDate), MONTH(OrderDate)
ORDER BY Year DESC, Month DESC;
```

Explanation:

- YEAR(OrderDate) and MONTH(OrderDate) extract the year and month from the OrderDate.
- SUM(TotalAmount) calculates the total sales for each month.
- COUNT(DISTINCT OrderID) counts the number of distinct orders placed in each month.
- The result is grouped by year and month and ordered in descending order to show the most recent months first.

Step 2: Sales by Product Category

Now, let's add the sales breakdown by product category. To do this, we need to join the `Orders` and `OrderDetails` tables with the `Products` table to access the product category.

sql

```sql
SELECT
    YEAR(o.OrderDate) AS Year,
    MONTH(o.OrderDate) AS Month,
    p.Category,
    SUM(od.Quantity     *     od.Price)     AS
SalesByCategory
FROM Orders o
INNER  JOIN  OrderDetails  od  ON  o.OrderID  =
od.OrderID
INNER  JOIN  Products  p  ON  od.ProductID  =
p.ProductID
GROUP BY YEAR(o.OrderDate), MONTH(o.OrderDate),
p.Category
ORDER BY Year DESC, Month DESC, SalesByCategory
DESC;
```

Explanation:

- This query joins the `Orders` and `OrderDetails` tables to get the `ProductID` and uses the `Products` table to fetch the `Category`.

243

- We calculate the total sales for each category by multiplying Quantity by Price for each order.
- The query groups results by year, month, and product category, and sorts the results by sales within each month.

Step 3: Total Number of Products Sold

To calculate the total number of products sold each month, we can aggregate the quantities from the OrderDetails table.

sql

```
SELECT
    YEAR(o.OrderDate) AS Year,
    MONTH(o.OrderDate) AS Month,
    SUM(od.Quantity) AS TotalProductsSold
FROM Orders o
INNER JOIN OrderDetails od ON o.OrderID =
od.OrderID
GROUP BY YEAR(o.OrderDate), MONTH(o.OrderDate)
ORDER BY Year DESC, Month DESC;
```

Explanation:

- We use SUM(od.Quantity) to calculate the total quantity of products sold each month.
- The query is grouped by year and month, similar to the previous queries.

244

Step 4: Combining Data for a Comprehensive Report

Finally, we can combine the results of the previous queries into a single comprehensive report. To do this, we use LEFT JOIN to combine the monthly sales, category sales, and product quantities.

sql

```
SELECT
     s.Year,
     s.Month,
     s.TotalSales,
     s.NumberOfOrders,
     c.SalesByCategory,
     p.TotalProductsSold
FROM
     (SELECT
         YEAR(OrderDate) AS Year,
         MONTH(OrderDate) AS Month,
         SUM(TotalAmount) AS TotalSales,
         COUNT(DISTINCT          OrderID)          AS
NumberOfOrders
     FROM Orders
     GROUP BY YEAR(OrderDate), MONTH(OrderDate))
s
LEFT JOIN
     (SELECT
         YEAR(o.OrderDate) AS Year,
```

```
    MONTH(o.OrderDate) AS Month,
    SUM(od.Quantity   *   od.Price)   AS
SalesByCategory
    FROM Orders o
    INNER JOIN OrderDetails od ON o.OrderID =
od.OrderID
    INNER JOIN Products p ON od.ProductID =
p.ProductID
    GROUP         BY          YEAR(o.OrderDate),
MONTH(o.OrderDate), p.Category) c
ON s.Year = c.Year AND s.Month = c.Month
LEFT JOIN
    (SELECT
        YEAR(o.OrderDate) AS Year,
        MONTH(o.OrderDate) AS Month,
        SUM(od.Quantity) AS TotalProductsSold
    FROM Orders o
    INNER JOIN OrderDetails od ON o.OrderID =
od.OrderID
    GROUP         BY          YEAR(o.OrderDate),
MONTH(o.OrderDate)) p
ON s.Year = p.Year AND s.Month = p.Month
ORDER BY s.Year DESC, s.Month DESC;
```

Explanation:

- This query combines the three queries we created earlier (total sales, category sales, and total products sold) using LEFT JOIN.

- Each part of the report is grouped by year and month, and we join the results based on the year and month.
- The final report contains the total sales, number of orders, sales by category, and total products sold for each month.

Step 5: Exporting Data for Visualization

Once the data is retrieved using SQL, it can be exported to tools like Excel, Power BI, or Tableau for visualization. For example, you can export the results of this query to a CSV file and use it to create bar charts, line graphs, or pie charts to visually present the sales data.

Summary

In this chapter, you learned how to use SQL for **data analysis and reporting**. We covered:

- How to aggregate data using SQL functions like `SUM()`, `COUNT()`, and `AVG()` to produce key metrics.
- Techniques for generating **complex reports** by joining multiple tables and using filtering and grouping.
- A real-world example of generating a **monthly sales report** for an e-commerce website, including total sales, sales by product category, and total products sold.
- How to prepare data for visualization by exporting it to external tools for further analysis.

By mastering these SQL techniques, you can efficiently analyze and report on large datasets, enabling data-driven decision-making and business insights.

CHAPTER 27

FUTURE OF SQL AND DATABASE TECHNOLOGIES

Evolving Trends in Databases (NoSQL, Cloud Databases, etc.)

The world of databases is rapidly evolving, and the landscape is shifting to accommodate the growing demand for scalability, flexibility, and performance in modern applications. While **SQL** and relational databases have been the backbone of data storage for decades, newer database technologies such as **NoSQL** and **cloud databases** have emerged to address challenges that relational databases were not originally designed to handle.

Let's explore some of the major trends that are shaping the future of databases:

1. NoSQL Databases

NoSQL (Not Only SQL) refers to a broad category of databases that do not use traditional relational database models. NoSQL databases are designed to handle unstructured, semi-structured, and large volumes of data in a way that is more scalable and flexible than traditional SQL databases. They are particularly well-suited for applications that require high availability, low latency, and the ability to handle massive datasets that do not fit neatly into relational tables.

Some common types of NoSQL databases include:

- **Document-based Databases** (e.g., MongoDB, CouchDB): Store data in documents, typically in JSON or BSON format. This allows for flexible schema designs.
- **Key-Value Stores** (e.g., Redis, DynamoDB): Store data as a collection of key-value pairs, which makes them fast and simple for certain use cases like caching.
- **Column-family Stores** (e.g., Cassandra, HBase): Organize data into columns, making them efficient for storing large amounts of data that need to be accessed quickly by column.
- **Graph Databases** (e.g., Neo4j, ArangoDB): Designed for handling data with complex relationships, such as social networks, recommendation systems, or fraud detection.

When to Use NoSQL:

- You need high scalability and performance for large-scale, high-velocity data (e.g., social media platforms, IoT applications).
- The data model is unstructured or semi-structured, making it difficult to enforce a rigid relational schema.

- You need low-latency access to massive datasets, such as for real-time applications.

2. Cloud Databases

Cloud computing has revolutionized how databases are hosted and managed. Cloud databases are hosted on cloud platforms like **Amazon Web Services (AWS)**, **Microsoft Azure**, and **Google Cloud**, providing flexibility, scalability, and ease of management. Cloud databases offer both relational (SQL) and non-relational (NoSQL) options.

Some advantages of cloud databases include:

- **Scalability**: Cloud databases can scale vertically (by increasing resources like CPU or memory) or horizontally (by adding more instances) as data grows.
- **Managed Services**: Cloud providers offer fully managed database services (e.g., Amazon RDS, Google Cloud SQL, Azure SQL Database) that handle patching, backups, and replication automatically.
- **High Availability**: Cloud databases are designed to be highly available, with built-in disaster recovery options and geographically distributed data centers.
- **Cost Efficiency**: Cloud databases use a pay-as-you-go pricing model, which allows businesses to scale their

database infrastructure based on current demand, without the need for significant upfront investment.

Cloud Database Examples:

- **Amazon Aurora**: A relational database service that is fully compatible with MySQL and PostgreSQL but offers better performance and scalability.
- **Google BigQuery**: A cloud data warehouse that is optimized for large-scale data analysis and reporting.
- **Microsoft Azure Cosmos DB**: A globally distributed, multi-model NoSQL database service that supports document, key-value, graph, and column-family data models.

3. Hybrid and Multi-Model Databases

Some modern database solutions are **multi-model**, meaning they combine multiple types of databases into one system, allowing you to handle different types of data (e.g., relational, document, key-value) with a single platform. These databases aim to provide the flexibility of NoSQL while maintaining the reliability and structure of SQL.

For example, **ArangoDB** supports graph, document, and key-value data models, allowing users to choose the best model for their use case. Similarly, **Couchbase** combines document, key-value, and SQL-like query capabilities in a single platform.

4. Serverless Databases

Serverless databases are a relatively new concept where the cloud provider automatically handles scaling and management of the database infrastructure. Users only pay for the resources they consume, and there is no need to manually manage database instances or clusters. This model is particularly useful for applications with variable workloads.

Example:

- **Amazon Aurora Serverless**: Automatically scales based on the number of requests and is a cost-effective option for variable workloads.

How SQL Fits into the Modern Tech Ecosystem

Despite the rise of NoSQL and cloud databases, **SQL** continues to play a critical role in the modern database ecosystem. Here's how SQL fits into the evolving landscape:

1. **Relational Databases Remain Core**: Relational databases, powered by SQL, are still the backbone of many business applications, particularly those that require strong consistency and transactional support. Many

253

enterprise systems (e.g., finance, healthcare) rely on relational databases because of their ability to maintain data integrity and enforce business rules.

2. **SQL in the Cloud**: Cloud providers continue to offer SQL databases as managed services, making it easier to deploy, scale, and maintain relational databases in the cloud. Examples include **Amazon RDS, Azure SQL Database**, and **Google Cloud SQL**.

3. **SQL in Big Data and Analytics**: SQL is still widely used in big data and analytics platforms, especially for querying structured data. Technologies like **Google BigQuery** and **Amazon Redshift** allow users to run SQL queries on massive datasets, making it easy to perform data analysis and generate reports.

4. **Hybrid Systems**: Many organizations are adopting hybrid systems that combine SQL and NoSQL databases. For example, SQL might be used for transactional data (e.g., customer orders), while NoSQL is used for managing large-scale, unstructured data (e.g., social media posts).

5. **SQL in Data Science and Machine Learning**: SQL is commonly used by data scientists to query data and prepare it for analysis, machine learning models, and data visualization. SQL is integrated into data pipelines that collect, process, and analyze data before feeding it into machine learning algorithms.

Real-World Example: Migrating an Existing Relational Database to a Cloud Platform

Let's assume you are working with a business that wants to migrate its existing on-premise SQL database to a cloud platform to take advantage of scalability, cost savings, and managed services.

Step 1: Assessing the Database

The first step in migration is to assess the current on-premise SQL database to understand its structure, size, performance requirements, and any potential challenges. Key questions include:

- What version of SQL is the database using?
- How large is the database, and what are the peak usage times?
- Are there any specific security or compliance requirements (e.g., GDPR)?
- What features (e.g., backups, replication) are critical for the business?

Step 2: Choosing the Right Cloud Database

Based on the assessment, you will select the appropriate cloud database service. For instance:

- **Amazon RDS for SQL Server**: If you are using SQL Server on-premise, Amazon RDS for SQL Server offers a fully managed database service that is compatible with your existing setup.
- **Amazon Aurora**: For MySQL or PostgreSQL-based databases, Amazon Aurora offers better performance and scalability with SQL compatibility.
- **Azure SQL Database**: For businesses already using Microsoft tools, Azure SQL Database offers seamless integration with the Microsoft ecosystem.

Step 3: Migrating Data

The next step is migrating the data to the cloud platform. This can be done using tools like:

- **AWS Database Migration Service (DMS)**: AWS DMS can migrate data from on-premise SQL databases to cloud-based databases with minimal downtime.
- **Azure Database Migration Service**: This service helps migrate databases from SQL Server, MySQL, or PostgreSQL to Azure SQL Database or other Azure-based solutions.

Step 4: Testing and Optimization

After migration, extensive testing is required to ensure that the database performs optimally in the cloud. Key areas to test include:

- Query performance and latency.
- Backup and restore processes.
- Security configurations.
- Scalability during peak loads.

Step 5: Monitoring and Maintenance

Once the migration is complete, ongoing monitoring and maintenance are crucial to ensure the database continues to perform well in the cloud. Cloud providers offer built-in monitoring tools to track performance, backups, and security.

Example Tools:

- **Amazon CloudWatch**: Monitors the performance of cloud-based SQL databases.
- **Azure Monitor**: Tracks the health and performance of Azure SQL Databases.

Summary

In this chapter, we explored the **future of SQL** and how new database technologies such as **NoSQL**, **cloud databases**, and **hybrid systems** are reshaping the landscape of data storage and management. Despite the rise of newer technologies, **SQL remains central** in the modern tech ecosystem for structured data management, big data analytics, and transactional systems.

We also discussed how to **migrate an existing relational database** to a cloud platform, highlighting the benefits of cloud services, including scalability, cost-effectiveness, and managed services. As businesses continue to adopt cloud platforms, SQL will remain an essential part of the database landscape, integrated with both traditional and emerging technologies.

By understanding these trends and migration strategies, you can future-proof your database architecture and take full advantage of cloud-based databases and modern data management practices.